Also by Jeannette R. Scollard

No-Nonsense Management Tips for Women

THE
SELF-EMPLOYED
WOMAN

How to Start Your Own Business and Gain Control of Your Life

Jeannette R.Scollard

Simon and Schuster • New York

Published by Simon and Schuster
A Division of Simon & Schuster, Inc.
Simon & Schuster Building
Rockefeller Center
1230 Avenue of the Americas
New York, New York 10020
SIMON AND SCHUSTER and colophon are registered trademarks
    of Simon & Schuster, Inc.
Designed by Levavi & Levavi
Manufactured in the United States of America
10 9 8 7 6 5 4 3 2 1
Library of Congress Cataloging in Publication Data
Scollard, Jeannette R.
    The self-employed woman.

    Includes index.
    1. New business enterprises.   2. Women in business.
3. Women-owned business enterprises.   I. Title.
HD62.5. S36   1985   658.4′2   85–14397
ISBN: 0-671-50084-8

For
Gary Scollard

Acknowledgments

This book would not have been possible without the cooperation of a remarkable breed of women who are entrepreneurs. They are an unusually candid and lively coterie. Interviewing them was an unmitigated delight.

Moreover, I am indebted to the specialists and experts who so generously contributed their insights and expertises to forearm all the self-employed women who are this book's readers.

My deepest gratitude goes to four women who sustained me throughout this undertaking: to Dottie Guyon for her loyal assistance; to Bridget McGonigle for her moral support; to Judith Moncrieff for her intelligent perspective; and to Jayne Pearl for her dedication and enthusiasm.

JRS

Contents

Preface

We are currently witnessing an important shift in the American workplace. In dramatically increasing numbers, women are rejecting traditional work in the male-dominated corporate world to venture into their own businesses. Women more than ever before are deciding to write their own rules, set their own hours, and pay their own salaries. This is the fascinating, incredibly challenging, and perilous world of the self-employed woman.

One-third of the approximately 1.5 million new corporations established in the United States last year were formed by women. Today there are already between three and four million entrepreneurial women in the business community, and millions more are actively contemplating becoming entrepreneurs and being their own bosses.

In a great groundswell American women are finally exploring the greatest personal freedom in our culture—freedom to control our own personal and business destinies. We are taking charge of our lives and becoming our own bosses, and we're loving it. This book, chapter by chapter, will take you through every phase of starting your own business, from that moment of truth when you decide to go it alone to planning for your comfortable and safe retirement. So read on and enjoy, and remember, with sufficient luck, determination, and planning, you too can become a successful and fulfilled entrepreneur—a self-employed woman.

The Moment of Truth

Prologue

Full-fledged entrepreneurs are rarely born, but made—by hard circumstance, thwarted career advancement, or just plain desire for increased business independence. Sometimes, unwillingly, women are *propelled* toward that moment—we call it "The Moment of Truth"—when they realize that they simply can no longer work for anyone else.

Arriving at this moment of truth for *you* may have been a long process full of stress. In the lives of women like you, who are considering going into business for themselves, there can be many unhappy months—or years—of dissatisfaction before you finally decide to take the entrepreneurial plunge. Perhaps you have been disappointed by your opportunities to advance in a corporate job, or distressed by the rigidity of your job's routine, or really bothered by the profound frustration of not feeling in control of your business life. On the other hand, your skills may be so undervalued in the traditional marketplace that there are simply no jobs worth your time and effort. Whether you are in the process of reevaluating a corporate job, or whether there are simply no acceptable jobs available for you in the preexisting business world, arriving at the conclusion that you should go out on your own is a weighty and complex decision. It should never be made in haste.

Making this decision, however, has many potential rewards. "My company is my name, my pride, and my life," declares Georgette Klinger, who owns a chain of skin care salons. "I love my company. I'm me. I'm wonderful," effuses designer and manufacturer Harriet Winter. These women exhibit the typical positiveness and ebullience of the successful self-employed woman.

But before you can experience the euphoria that accompanies successful entrepreneurship, you must deal with a variety of stresses and decisions. This book will teach you how to cope with the stress—and how to make the *right* decisions.

CHAPTER ONE

The Stress of a Corporate Job

Working for someone else, be it another person, a small company, or a huge corporation, is sometimes wonderful. You love your job, it is challenging, you like the people you work with and are generally satisfied with your situation. If this is true, and your present job suits you to a T, congratulate yourself that you are one of the few lucky Americans who has found a match of personality and job situation.

Unfortunately, many women discover that after a bright beginning in a new job or in a particular field, they are stymied in their careers. Knowing there is no place to go can be extremely demoralizing. You might initially feel restless and discontented in this unhappy situation, then you may begin to dread facing your job. Repetitive tasks may bore you intensely, and you may have to face the reality that in ten to twenty years you'll arrive at your job and be doing exactly the same things—tasks that long ago ceased to excite you. You have arrived at a dead end. This realization can create enormous personal stress.

"I hated to go to work every morning," recalls Laurie Malcom, who reached a dead-end position as a technician in a hospital. "I hated my work, and everybody around me hated theirs." Malcom routinely suffered bouts of despair. She was so dissatisfied with her job that it influenced her attitude about everything. She says, "The things that used to make me happy didn't make me happy anymore."

The stress caused by a dead-end job can be a major factor in your decision to become an entrepreneur.

Malcom realized that she had to change her life. She began by taking courses in insurance in the evenings as preparation for a change. Today she heads up her own insurance brokerage firm in Boston. "I would never work for anyone again," she says.

Women Continue to Be Discriminated Against in Corporate America.

No matter how good you are at what you do, the higher you climb the American corporate hierarchy, the more likely you are to be thwarted by prejudice and dead-ended in a job below your maximum potential. Unless you are in one of the few industries in which women have made inroads into management, such as advertising, publishing, and fashion, male-dominated corporate America simply is not yet prepared to accept you as the president or chief executive officer—or even as the sales manager or operations vice-president. Sadly, this movement to the top is simply not happening.

One woman, outstanding in her field and the obvious choice to be chief of her company, was told by her male managers, "We know you're the best. We would make you president, but the company would then be the laughingstock of the industry. No one would take us seriously." Up against a dead end in her career, the woman turned entrepreneur: she is now a high-priced consultant to the industry.

Although it is depressing and illegal, discrimination remains a fact of life in much of American business. Columbia Business School's Mary Anne Devanna observes, "Part of the reason there is an increasing number of female entrepreneurs is that some of the corporate channels are still blocked to them."

Unfortunately, we've got a long way to go before we have an equal chance across the board with men. "Women have not risen to equal respect in our society," observes Mary Kay Ash. "Things haven't changed very much for women. It is still a man's world. Women today still have a hard time." Mary Kay Cosmetics is, of course, one of the great American success stories. Ash says that she realized when she started her cosmetics business over twenty years ago there was no chance she would get into the executive suite of any company she didn't own. "They said, 'Mary Kay, you're thinking like a woman,' to put me down," she recalls. "I used that to our advantage," she adds, smiling.

"The struggle for women is not past. We're still in it in a major way," notes Merry Clark, editor of *Sunday Woman,* a nationally syndicated weekly newspaper supplement with a circulation of four million.

"I'm surrounded by male chauvinist pigs," admits an executive at a communications firm. "Give them a drink or two among themselves and what they really think about women comes pouring out. They don't like us when we tell them what to do."

Reports Muriel Siebert, who heads up a Wall Street firm bearing her name, "There's still no ladies' room at the luncheon club at the New York Stock Exchange. You have to go to another floor." Though relatively minor in itself, this is indicative of the lack of progress women have made into the most powerful of all circles— the world of finance. Not *one* single woman is an important partner in any major Wall Street firm. No one woman is in line to run a major bank; women are routinely rebuffed in conservative financial organizations.

What can you do if you're rejected by male management in your field? You do just what Venita vanCaspel did after having been continually rebuffed by the male establishment at a Houston brokerage firm. "They wouldn't seat me in out in the middle but gave me a desk on the far side of the room in the corner," vanCaspel relates. She launched her own firm, which is now too large and successful to be ignored by the community that initially snubbed her.

Corporate Life Can Be Defeminizing.

A management consultant recalls how she used to compromise to fit into the style of a large corporation. "When I was working for a company, I was competing with all the guys for attention. I deliberately defeminized myself to be competitive, playing the game by their rules. I looked very different and I felt very different about myself. I felt I was drowning. I felt I was losing my own identity. Now that I'm on my own I don't have to compete in the same way. Now I'm definitely more feminine. I look more feminine. I think more feminine."

As we've implied, corporations become increasingly male-dominated as you near the top, and the corporate game in most companies does in fact tend to force women to conform to men's rules to win. You dress to blend in. In some industries it is still necessary to wear suits and carry a briefcase. In conservative businesses such as steel and heavy machinery, a woman may feel uncomfortable wearing eye makeup to the office.

Whatever the circumstances, a woman must dress to conform because she does not want to be perceived primarily as a sex object. You take care not to call attention to your sexuality. You want men to focus on your excellence, not on your attractiveness. You want them to think about you as a candidate for the president's chair, not as a candidate for sexual conquest. To accomplish this, you may have to defeminize yourself deliberately. For instance, a woman I met while researching this book who has spectacularly beautiful long hair always wore it in a severe bun at the office until she started her own business. Now she wears it down—as *she* likes it.

Interestingly, the beauty and femininity that work *against* you when you are employed at a company can work *for* you once you move outside the traditional structure. "The corporations will buy my feminine input from the outside. But inside I would never have been this successful," observes the consultant. Notes another woman who moved from employment by a big corporation to providing consulting services as an entrepreneur, "Being beautiful means I make a more dramatic impact when I make a presentation. Being attractive makes me a better salesperson of my own abilities. It never worked for me when I was employed by the corporation."

Salaried Jobs Can Be Dreary.

I have also noticed a marked difference in the work-related conversations of groups of women who are employed by businesses they do not own and those who are entrepreneurs: salaried women tend to complain about their jobs, and most of them are dissatisfied. How often do you meet someone who has the perfect job? On the other hand, the women who have their own businesses most often are much happier and more buoyant about their prospects.

As an employee you have more to complain about because you may be an insignificant cog in a giant machine. Your talents may be largely unused and unappreciated. You may be assigned to tasks you find rote and meaningless. Your objectives may be set at the whim of management. Your ideas may be routinely stolen by your boss.

Even if you are high ranking in your organization, you may still be bored. A Realtor who previously held a prized job at one of the country's largest corporations notes, "I left because it was impersonal and lonely. It just wasn't ever fun." Now she says her work experience is "rich and wonderful—and it pays."

Further, you may have to play political games to maintain your footing in a company where you are employed. You may spend a large portion of your energy plotting how to get ahead. Gamesmanship is a serious pastime in big corporations.

You Have No Control over Your Work—When, Where, What It Is, or with Whom.

Your job's structure probably allows you little freedom to choose or vary your hours. You are given certain times to report to a given place to perform tasks that may vary according to the needs of your boss, and your associates are determined by the job and not by your choice. The lack of control over all these factors can create great problems for you.

When—If you are like most employees, you work the standard nine to five. This means that you are going to work and coming home at the same time as everyone else in your time zone. You commute at peak hours and you all are in the checkout line of the grocery store with everyone else. This in itself can be frustrating.

But it can be the confinement of a nine-to-five workday that you find most trying. If you are the sort of person who prefers working twelve-hour days seven days a week on a project until it is completed and then taking a break, a nine-to-five schedule can be very frustrating. Or you may be the sort to finish your work in record time, but then must sit at your desk with nothing to do because you are obliged to be on the job at least eight hours a day, regardless of how you pace your work.

All this changes when you run your own business. You operate it to suit your inclinations. You may work twelve hours and take off the afternoon of the next day. Perhaps you work twenty days in a row and then spend five days at your country house relaxing. Or maybe you continue to work forty hours a week, but the hours are of your own choosing.

Where—Your employer probably demands that you perform your duties in a specific place. If you are an office worker, you must work at your desk. Your office environment may not be conducive to your doing your best work, but your job requires that you be there anyway to complete all tasks.

By contrast, as an entrepreneur you can decide where to do your work. You can take your paperwork home—and have your secretary come there, too. For instance, a public relations expert has her staff report in to her country home for five days of the week during the summer—Tuesdays and Wednesdays are spent at the office.

What your work is—If you work for someone, you do the work that you are given. Whether it is what you do best is often not a consideration. Whether or not you like the work is almost never a factor. No matter how inconsequential or boring, you do the work your boss assigns you. This can create enormous depression and stress if the work does not challenge you and give you a sense of self-worth and accomplishment.

When you start your own business you can choose work that for you is interesting and enjoyable. Thus, if you dislike working with sick people, you could go into life insurance sales—where only healthy people are eligible customers. If you hate sitting in an office, you should find a business that requires you to be active and away from a desk.

Whom you work with—As an employee you are required to work with whoever has already been hired. You do not have to like them or respect them, nor they you. You must, however, work together. If you like your colleagues and boss, your work is much more pleasant. Indeed, you may like the people you work with so much that you look forward to seeing them every day. But if you dislike them, and the environment is fraught with dirty politics and hostility, there is little you can do except look for another job and hope you find a more congenial crew.

The only way you can really control the people with whom you associate is if you have the option of turning down work that necessitates your dealing with unpleasant people, and the only way you have that option is if you own the company.

Criticism Can Create Stress.

Being an employee also means that someone is watching and evaluating your performance. The technique with which tasks are performed and your own personal style are also under scrutiny. You may be criticized for being too soft when your boss believes you should be more forceful, and vice versa.

If you make a mistake, you must account for it, and the ultimate punishment for making a mistake is losing your job. Living under the fear of being wrong and getting fired can make you miserably insecure. But if you are a conscientious person, failure is often in itself punishment enough. Only if you are an entrepreneur do you have the freedom to fail without receiving flak. "I hated being reminded that I failed and having to explain," states a woman who went into competition with her previous employer. "Now if I mess up, I take the blame, and that's all there is to it."

Your Energy Can Be Wasted.

Employed by someone else, your day may be filled with energy-sapping tasks. Not only politics may be a major preoccupation in your office, but your enthusiasm for your work may be buried under paperwork and bureaucracy. You may have to spend more effort getting your managers to approve a project than it takes to complete the undertaking. You may be assigned to meaningless committees where mandatory meetings are long and little is accomplished. You may report to managers who are terrified of making a decision—after you have spent months gathering information to form a basis of the decisions you propose.

In short, you may feel that you are expending substantial energy without achieving substantive results.

This can make entrepreneurship look more attractive to you. There are no committees; you make all the decisions and there is no bureaucracy whatsoever. When you have your own business your energy can be directed solely toward quickly achieving your objectives.

Your Family Responsibilities Can Be at Odds with Your Job.

Chances are that your job and your family are two different worlds, each with great demands and responsibilities. On the one hand, you work the hours and days that are assigned to you in your career; then you must scramble to meet the needs of your husband and children. This juggling act can make you frantic. For instance, school hours usually do not coincide with your work hours, and school vacations are far longer than the vacations your job permits. Thus you have the burden of making arrangements to care for your children in your absence. Moreover, as wife and mother you usually bear the lion's share of responsibilities for the care and feeding of your family. In fact, the joint demands of job and family may leave little time for you to have any fun.

At your office you may feel it is best to downplay the importance of your family in your life because it may be detrimental to advancement. You don't want to be denied the opportunity to head up a difficult project that could lead to a promotion simply because of your family obligations.

Struggling to be superwoman—the perfect employee in addition to being a good wife and mother—can be excruciating. Even if you are able to manage all three roles, often you find there is no time left for yourself. The end result is that you are privately frazzled and frustrated because you simply cannot do everything.

This is another reason women become entrepreneurs. Entrepreneurship can allow you a more relaxed family life. You are able to adjust your work schedule to meet the family's needs. For instance, Anne Hoffman opted out of a high-powered corporate job and chose real estate sales because it was a career that provided her with flexibility to meet the needs of her children while they were growing up. "What kind of work you choose is a critical factor in how you can adapt your working life to fit with your family life," she observes.

But regardless of the nature of your business, if you are in control of it, you can make adjustments to meet your family's demands. Georgette Klinger deliberately postponed national expansion of her beauty care salons until her daughter had gone off to college, because the expansion would have required long absences from home. Moreover, as an entrepreneur, you can schedule your work load around your family, planning vacations as needed. You can turn down a contract or order that would be particularly disruptive to your family's schedule; you can control which times your work will be most demanding. In short, you can avoid some of the stress that comes from the continual conflict between home and work.

What If You Are Smarter than Your Boss?

When you start out working for a company, you may assume that the management of it knows more than you do about their business. But as you become more experienced you may realize you are beginning to know a great deal more than the senior management. "I used to think the guys at the top were smart. I found out, the higher I went, that they didn't know very much at all. They simply bluffed their way through," notes a former executive who now consults for her previous employer.

Once you realize that you know at least as much as your boss, you tend privately to begin to second-guess his or her decisions and itch for a greater role in the decision-making process. Of course, often your own judgment is proven better than your boss's.

Then you become irritated at the time that could have been saved if you had been listened to.

Once you gain confidence in your own judgment, the temptation to make your own decisions becomes strong. You realize that if you had your own firm, you could avoid many of the problems your boss routinely encounters. You learn that you could fare well if you were the one in charge.

You Are Rewarded Indirectly.

When you are clever and save the company you work for thousands of dollars, the company benefits—not you. If you are lucky, you may be able to persuade your boss to give you a raise the next time your salary is reviewed. Sometimes your *best* efforts result in great savings for the company, but your efforts are never even acknowledged. If you call your work to the attention of your superiors, you may be told, "Cutting costs is part of your job." So much for being rewarded.

One of the most satisfying things about running your own business is that the rewards of your ingenuity and labor come to you directly in the form of profits. If you negotiate a discount, the savings are reflected immediately. The extra effort you put out is immediately felt by the extra success your venture achieves.

"It's more fun when I'm right and my company benefits than it was when I was right and working for someone else," notes Anne Ready, who heads up Ready for Media in Los Angeles. "Before, the people I worked for got all the benefits and all I got was a pat on the head—if that."

When you run your own life, it's very simple. You profit when you're good. You lose when you're not.

CHAPTER TWO

There Is a Way Out

Degrees and traditional scholastic credentials mean more in the corporate arena than does life experience and nonbusiness expertise. Therefore, if you have been working as a full-time mother and housewife, you may discover when you try to get a job working for a company that you are able to enter only at the lowliest clerical level. You may have run a complex household and the schedules of a half dozen family members, but when you look for a job you're only fit to run the Xerox machine: you have no "business experience." All you are qualified to be is a receptionist or a clerk.

What can you do?

One of your options outside of the clerical pool is to move out of the traditional workplace. By focusing on your unique skills, insight, and knowledge, you may use them to start your own business.

This is easier said than done. It is difficult to focus on precisely what you have to offer that could be the basis of a successful business. Finding the particular service or product that will be your vehicle to success can be stressful, too. And often it is difficult to decide how best to package your skills.

What If You Think You Have Nothing to Offer?

You may need to go to work, but you may feel your skills are not valued in the marketplace. You may lack a college education, business experience, or any kind of special training. Still, believe it or not, there is always something you can find to do.

Honey Levine in New Jersey found herself with four small children to support after the sudden death of her husband. "I had no formal education, no training, and no experience. I couldn't just march into any company because I didn't know how to do anything," Levine recalls. She decided to rely on her demonstrated skill to get along with people. This enabled her to become very successful selling real estate. Says Levine, who now owns a Century 21 franchise in New Jersey, "In the first year I reached my goal of being able to support my family. . . ." The second year she reached $1 million in sales.

If you are a resourceful wife and mother, you already possess some very special skills. You routinely orchestrate parties for the family, decorate your home, meet people at the airport, and generally organize the lives of several people. This in itself is a marketable commodity. Elizabeth Woolf developed Renta Yenta to do all the things for other people she had long been doing for her family. "We do not do anything anyone could not do themselves with proper research and logic and thinking and time," Woolf says. "But we're dealing with people who are too lazy or too busy."

You can take a basic home skill that you enjoy and capitalize on it on a part-time basis. You can do as does Patti McLain of Cruz Bay, St. John. She sews imaginative stuffed animals and festively decorated kitchen accessories to sell at Christmastime. She enjoys creating them and they are very profitable, but she resists requests to supply merchants on a year-round basis. "If I had to do it all the time, I'm afraid it might stop being fun," she observes.

The fact is women have been supporting their families and supplementing their incomes for centuries doing "woman's work." They have scrubbed floors for hire, taken in boarders and fed them and cleaned their rooms, and baby-sat for their neighbors. They have sewn clothes, knitted sweaters, and cooked for hire. You too can turn any of these skills into a viable business.

Kitchen Skills Can Be Your Entrée.

You probably learned to cook at your mother's knee and have been doing it very capably all your adult years. But the products you routinely produce in your kitchen can be the source of a new business. You can make salad dressings, grow herbs and make vinegars, or bake cakes and sell them to stores and restaurants. You can do what Jessie Cibelli did in Lenox, Massachusetts. Born in Scotland, she came to America and worked as a housekeeper and nanny before becoming a full-time housewife. Cibelli was known among her friends for her excellent Scottish shortbread. She started baking it to sell a couple of years ago, working out of her daughter's basement. She made about $15,000 the first year, plowing everything back into the business to buy a convection oven, a larger mixer, and packing machines. The shortbread is increasingly successful, and Cibelli's future as a baker seems very promising.

Usually you begin your cooking endeavors right in your own kitchen. But before you begin there are two important factors to consider. First, state laws vary: check yours to see exactly what the health codes are, and be certain you are not prohibited from cooking commercially in your family kitchen. Also, be aware that some large stores require that you obtain product liability insurance before they will purchase food from you.

Specialized Training Can Be Resold.

If you know how to do something most other people do not know, you can sell that information. You can set up either a consulting firm or a training school. For instance, Zsuzsi Starkloff of Columbus, Ohio, who had trained as a pilot to overcome her fear of flying, found the skill useful after she divorced and needed to make money. She founded Starflite, an accelerated school for qualifying people to obtain a commercial pilot's license and instrument-rating skills. What takes six months to a year to learn in conventional schools, Starkloff teaches her students in two weeks. Says Starkloff, "I figured that if I had to work, why not work at something I loved?"

What you know and sell can be much less esoteric. You might teach a foreign language if you're fluent in one. If you have a knack in a special field, you can teach it to paying students. Claudia Carr was first a savvy, highly organized waitress. Friends who admired the way Carr managed a restaurant in Sun Valley, Idaho, asked her to train their staffs and set up restaurant procedures in new ventures. Word of mouth led to more restaurant owners requesting her assistance, and Carr discovered she had a viable new business consulting.

Sometimes a tangential occupation associated with your field of expertise becomes your future business. St. John, U.S. Virgin Islands–based Gwen Byer discovered massage when she was a professional bike racer in Florida. "I always had a massage before and after every race. I loved it." Byer eventually went to massage school, studying with sports therapists in Michigan and a bush doctor in Trinidad, where she learned folk medicine to soothe strained muscles with herbs. Today she has a thriving private massage practice.

Your Hobby Can Become Your Business.

It is important to enjoy the work your business requires, because if you like it, you will be better at it—and happier doing it. Since your hobbies are presumably things you very much enjoy, you should consider pursuing one of them as a business. For example, if you enjoy sailboats, you can hire out yourself and your boat for charter passengers. That is what Jean Mason did along with her husband, John. For a dozen years they created *Fantasy Island* for their guests, including champagne and caviar lunches on deserted beaches, replete with crystal and linen tablecloths. Based in the Virgin Islands, they for many years guided their guests around the most remote islands on their fifty-six-foot sailboat. They never lost their love of sailing. Even though they are now retired, they continue to sail with undampened enthusiasm.

Ann Clark considered cooking a "passionate hobby" for many years. She routinely collected cookbooks in France and cooked two or three hours every evening when she returned from her job as a rare-print restorer. "I didn't realize I had acquired a skill," recalls Clark, who was extremely reluctant to give a cooking class for her friends in 1973. But during that first class Clark suddenly realized that she in fact had a great deal to offer. She immediately invested $500 to rent a space, two tables, and a dozen stools and opened LaBonne Cuisine School in Austin, Texas. From the first day her new undertaking was profitable.

Even off-beat hobbies can be the base of a viable business. Christine Rakela was interested in astrology and did readings through an agency to sustain herself as she pursued a career as a dancer. "Then I broke my foot and didn't know if I would be able to dance again," says Rakela. Her foot healed fine, but Rakela was already in the psychic business to stay. She founded her own agency, the Wizard of Results. It supplies practitioners of esoteric crafts for parties.

Initially modest undertakings can blossom if you are genuinely interested in what you are doing. Seventeen years ago housewife Ona Sommers opened a small shop in Des Moines, Iowa, to provide an outlet for creative women in the area to sell their handiwork. She sold their merchandise on consignment and kept the shop open only in the afternoon from one until four. Now all four of her children are grown and the shop is larger and open all day. Sommers finds other housewives eager to help her staff it. "Affluent women work for me as a way to blow off steam," observes Sommers, who is married to a dentist.

Types of Businesses You Might Consider If You Are a Novice
A service business with only you to staff it
A small retail business employing only one or two people
A business you can operate from your home to test your concept
A business with simple bookkeeping and accounting procedures
A business where you get paid promptly
A business requiring only a small inventory
A business doing something you know well and enjoy

Remember, keep it simple.

Types of Businesses to Avoid If You Are a Novice
Manufacturing operations
Companies that need large staffs or lots of employees
Businesses that require large amounts of space and rentals
Businesses that typically experience cash flow problems
Businesses where the accounting is complicated
Complex businesses
Businesses with heavy equipment and expensive machinery
A new business that has never been tried
A retread of a business that routinely fails
A business in an intensely competitive arena
A business connected with a fad

Keep Any New Undertaking Simple.

You are most likely to succeed if your first encounter with the business world is in as simple an operation as possible. Opening a day care center or a sewing shop is a relatively uncomplicated operation. They are both businesses where *you* provide the service. You have no employees. Office space is not essential for you to begin operations, although you may elect to relocate your business after you establish yourself. Meanwhile, you've kept your overhead down.

Further, you should select a business where you can judge exactly how well you are doing from month to month. You do not want to be surprised after six months to discover that you are not doing well—you want to be able to ascertain your progress easily all along.

Ideally you can finance your company the same way that Patricia Duncanson did when she and her husband started Duncanson Electric Co., an electrical contracting firm. "Our philosophy was that each job should pay for itself—it's important to strategize that," says Duncanson. "So I drew up our contract agreements so they would be paid in three installments, which set up our cash flow so we wouldn't have to use outside sources. That helped us gradually get credibility with our suppliers—they're a source of credit, of course." Duncanson's husband is an electrician, and she handles the administrative side of the company, which has grown consistently since they founded it in 1977.

When you are first considering the kind of business to open, you, too, should not spread yourself too thin. Specialize. Offer a service you can handle without attempting to be all things to all people. If you want to consult about art, don't try to include antiques, and vice versa. If you want to open a small snack bar, don't be tempted to add dinners until you have the snack bar operation fully in hand.

Do not lose sight of your original idea once you have convinced yourself you are right, but on the other hand, don't overestimate yourself. Even experienced, savvy business people fail. As a business person just starting out, you are far more vulnerable to failure.

Look Before You Leap.

Quietly investigate a number of ventures before you choose one. Visit other people who are already in the business and learn what their problems are and how they deal with them. Search out people who were unable to successfully open businesses in an area that interests you. Interview them and learn why they failed and how to avoid those problems. Steer clear of any business that doesn't work for a lot of people.

While you study the profitability and feasibility of a business, don't forget the value of your time. Figure out how much you can realistically make per hour for your labor in any venture. Calculate whether the rewards merit the risks.

Try to have as few illusions as possible about a business before you enter it. You might even try developing two scenarios: a *Worst Possible Case* and a *Best Possible Case*. Think about how you would perform in either instance, but expect your proposed venture to fall somewhere in between.

Do not act in haste. Becoming an entrepreneur is nothing to rush into. It means you receive no salary, no benefits, no office, and no support system unless you can supply it for yourself. Moreover, when you take the step to start, you are committed to taking certain risks, and whenever there are risks there is a high potential for failure. Deliberate at length before you decide to go into business for yourself. However, if you decide to take this great step, you should know that you also may experience some of the most rewarding and exciting professional and personal moments of your life.

CHAPTER THREE

How to Build Your Confidence

Even if you've had it with your dead-end job working for someone else, and you've started to outline careful plans for your own business, you may experience considerable trepidation about venturing out on your own. Indeed, you may conclude the risks are simply too great. But if you really believe you are ready to be your own boss, there are ways to buoy your spirits and increase your confidence.

By investigating the business you're considering thoroughly and building a network of contacts, you can gather enough information to give you an excellent idea of your prospects as an entrepreneur—before you launch your enterprise. But the really critical element of beginning your business successfully is self-knowledge—and self-confidence. You must be sure you are absolutely candid with yourself when you're getting started.

Assess Yourself.

Lengthy self-examination should precede your transition into entrepreneurship. You should assess the exact nature of the risks involved and decide if you are psychologically prepared to deal with the uncertainties as well as the headaches that inevitably accompany a new undertaking.

To accurately judge whether you are up to handling a business, of course, you must first thoroughly investigate it. You must know as much about a proposed undertaking as anyone who has not actually run it can know before you begin.

You also should decide exactly what you want out of life and how much time you are willing to devote. Perhaps you want a small venture, maybe even part-time, with virtually no downside. Or you may want to build a sizable company, beginning with a substantial investment. The stresses and headaches of a business directly relate to the ambitions you harbor for it. If you have big dreams of success, you must be prepared to work harder than you ever imagined and to endure periods of intense stress as you steer your business in a changing world of stiff competition. However, even running a small business can be time-consuming and difficult, and before you begin you must be sure owning your own business is really what you want to do.

Something else you must consider is the sheer amount of time your new business will require. When you are estimating the time a new venture will consume, you must add another 25 percent. There is usually more work entailed in starting any business than you initially anticipate. Be prepared in advance to work that extra 25 percent.

Do Something You Really Enjoy.

Under no circumstances should you venture into a business that has many aspects you do not particularly like. The whole point of becoming an entrepreneur is to take complete charge of your life and have the freedom to do what you want. Although no business is without a few irksome tasks, you should thoroughly enjoy the main thrust of your proposed undertaking. Moreover, if you love the area you are going into, you are more likely to learn about it and develop a "feel" for it. If you find the business exciting and challenging, you are more willing to spend the time and energy necessary to make it work.

Entrepreneurship can be fun sometimes, but it is mostly hard work, and there will be days when you'll wonder if you made the right decision launching your own business. But if you truly enjoy the business, you are far more likely to stick with it and have the persistence it takes to become a success.

Build a Network.

Before you begin any new venture, talk to as many people as you can in the business. Spend time observing precisely how their operations are conducted. Further, you should develop friendships with other entrepreneurs and budding entrepreneurs in order to share your misgivings and to problem-solve. You will find that you have a special rapport because you are all in the same boat together. People who have salaried jobs often cannot comprehend the anxiety and excitement of the entrepreneurial life-style. One woman who left a structured corporate life for a successful consulting career reports that she is gradually seeking out a whole new set of friends. "My old friends perpetually complain about their jobs and they simply live on another planet from me now," she says.

Seek out other women in similar circumstances who are already in the same business you are considering. Find out how it blends with their personal lives. Moreover, investigate the trade association for your proposed business and attend some of its meetings prior to starting your undertaking. There is no better way to get a feel for the exact nature of the business you are considering—and no easier way to find new friends.

By consciously building a network while you are planning your business, you build a wealth of support and information. In addition, you remove yourself from the position of reinventing the wheel—you can all learn from other business people's mistakes.

Set Realistic Goals.

It is very important to set reasonable goals and to have *realistic* expectations about your business's performance. If your expectations are too high, you are more likely to become discouraged and frustrated. Remember to plan your business conservatively—if it does better than you expected, you have only a happy surprise in store!

After you have done all your homework, sit down with a pen and some paper and write exactly what your expectations are for three months, six months, the first year, and the second year. Keep this piece of paper. As you begin your company your original estimates of your success can act as a touchstone to help you see how on track you are.

If it is a new business you are starting, you will usually have a hard time projecting beyond two years. You can *guess* what it will be in five years. But there is really no way of knowing exactly what kind of an entity you are creating until after you have been running it for a while.

Whenever you meet a projection, telephone two of your close friends and share the news of your achievement with them. Their congratulations will lift your spirits. Also share your success with someone you know who has had a similar business for a few years—that person can *really* appreciate what you have accomplished.

Be Patient.

Patience is also a vital part of entrepreneurship. You will not be able to force your business to blossom. You have to position yourself as carefully as possible in the business world and develop your company as circumstances permit. And once begun, a business takes on a life of its own. Trying to force it to grow too fast is a major reason many small business entrepreneurs fail. You have to be well informed, infinitely patient, a hard worker, and a little bit lucky to build a big company.

But once you decide that you have definitely become entrepreneurial material and have found the right niche for yourself, do not dissipate your energy by second-guessing yourself. Move cautiously, but don't get stymied by self-doubt and indecisiveness. Once you decide to go for it, give it your all!

Keep a Low Profile.

While you are planning your business, don't boast about it or publicly predict great things for it. First of all, as you investigate it more thoroughly, you may change your mind and decide it is not for you. Then, when you pursue another undertaking, the people who know you will be less likely to take you seriously—particularly your family and friends, whose support is most valuable to you. Quietly do your initial homework. After you have definitely decided to proceed and have laid some of the groundwork, you can announce it. But downplay the success you expect. One of the best ways to gain confidence is to exceed the expectations of the people around you.

Remember, however, when you're keeping this low profile, to believe in yourself. You may not receive a great deal of support from others during this time of contemplation and consolidation, and you must rely on yourself. As an entrepreneur, your business is you, and you *must* believe in yourself. Ultimately it is your confidence in you—your judgment and your capabilities—that will strengthen your business and make it a success. Keep in mind that you *can* do it—with knowledge and planning—as thousands of women every year are discovering.

Getting Started: Strategies for Success; Strategies for Succeeding Financially

Once you have arrived at that moment of truth when you decide you are destined to be an entrepreneur, you must face the enormous challenge of starting up a company. Important decisions must be made, and you want to make the right ones.

The first thing you need to determine is how you are going to raise the money to enable you to begin. This takes a great deal of preparation. But the information in the following pages will prepare you to deal with your banker and gird you against the possibility of failure.

You also must decide whether to get an office or start out at home, whether to hire an employee or to get a partner. You will have to finance your venture and perhaps land a bank loan to get started. You must learn how to pace yourself, and finally—how not to overextend yourself and fail.

Then, too, you should consider whether to buy an existing business instead of starting one from the ground up. You should weigh the advantages of opening the business with the safety net that the franchise provides you.

All these decisions are absolutely critical to your future. You are wise to inform yourself before you begin.

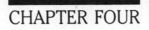

CHAPTER FOUR

Homework to Prepare You to Raise Money

No matter how you organize your business, you need to raise some cash to get it started. Going about getting money in a professional way will take careful preparation. The time you spend studying key financial concepts and numbers is well spent because these aspects of your business are its very soul. How well you handle your finances will ultimately determine whether or not you are successful.

Before you can talk about raising money to fund your company, you need to analyze the prospects of your business in a way that bankers and other financially oriented people can relate to.

You should familiarize yourself with the business terms. Doing your homework is important. The following two sections will explain the terms you must know to begin to analyze your profit potential and start-up costs.

Analyze Your Profit Potential.

You will never be able to raise money to start your business if you cannot convince your backers that the company will be profitable.

To determine if a proposed company can be profitable, you must analyze your financial prospects carefully. Examine the short-term financial costs and evaluate the long-term financial gains. If you are new to a business, you should consult people who are already operating companies in related areas and try to ascertain exactly how much money and effort will be required to break even.

Do your homework or you can get burned. A woman who was in the construction business and was forced out of it because of her inability to compete recalls: "I've been taken advantage of because I was financially naive. I gave away my profits to realtors. I was easily conned and I gave too much profit to my silent partners." Older and wiser, the woman vows never to begin another business without adequate planning and financial organization. Besides learning from her hard knocks, the former construction business owner is taking courses in finance. You, too, would be wise to attend business classes or carefully school yourself in the basics.

Architect Lynn Wilson plunged into her business headfirst when she began an interior design firm in 1970. "I didn't research the competition, start-up costs, overhead, or all the things you're supposed to do. If I had, I would've been scared to death and never would've started my company. I just jumped in, got $200 out of my bank account, and with my first retainer had a lawyer set up my incorporation." She was bright and creative enough to succeed despite her deliberately reckless beginnings. Creative Environs, her company, is one of the largest in the country that specializes in interiors for restaurants and clubs and other "hospitality" facilities. Wilson had three things working in her favor. She had her credentials—she trained as an architect. She could start off working from her home, making it possible to operate on a shoestring. But the most important factor was luck: Wilson was very lucky. Many women who start out as she did fail.

Estimate Your Start-up Costs.

The steeper your start-up costs, the harder it may be to raise enough money to begin. The simpler your undertaking, the easier it is to get it off the ground.

Whatever your start-up costs are projected to be, expect them to be substantially more. A retail shop owner says she tends to underestimate costs in almost every category. It cost more per square foot than she figured to build shop space, for instance. "I underestimated the specifics, too," she admits. "I estimated the air-conditioning system would cost about $25,000. It cost $40,000. I estimated the stereo system would cost $3,000. It cost $8,000." Her total cost overruns for the new shop she built were about $100,000. Fortunately she had other thriving stores and a friendly banker to make up the difference between what she projected and what she actually had to pay. An entrepreneur without her financial cushion would have been forced to sell out or go bankrupt.

To avoid underestimating, you should *add 20 percent to all your projected costs.* Generally, experienced entrepreneurs say that is a satisfactory safety net. It's much better to be left with extra cash on hand than to be caught short.

Comparison of Some of the Different Costs to Start Companies

(excluding paying yourself a salary and assuming you handle many of the responsibilities of selling, promoting, and providing the essential labor)

Type of Business	Kinds of Expenses	Estimated Minimum
Catering, small scale	Serving trays, appliances, extra refrigeration and storage, kitchen, phone (transportation not included)	$2,000
Catering, dinner up to fifty people	Serving trays, appliances to handle cooking,	$10,000

Type of Business	Kinds of Expenses	Estimated Minimum
	warming, extra refrigeration, storage containers, kitchen phone (van or station wagon not included)	
PR business	Phone, travel, brochure, attendance at trade shows to be visible, letterhead, stationery, and secretarial services	$25,000 first year
Mail order	Advertising of goods, initial inventory shipping and handling	$5,000
Gift shop	Six-month lease, utilities and phone, insurance, inventory	$200,000
Creative consultant, writer, editor, designer, decorator	Telephone, stationery, business cards, press releases	$100–$500
Chauffeur	Car, telephone and someone to answer 24 hours a day, business cards	$15,000–$20,000
Bake shop	Invoices, business cards (transportation not included)	$200–$500
Knit goods	Yarn, business cards	$1,000–$2,000
Newsletter	Paper and printing, editorial content, mailing list, postage, folding and addressing personnel	$50,000–$500,000
Cleaning service	Cleaning supplies, business cards (transportation not included)	$500
Plant maintenance	Business cards, hoses, plant foods, and lawn	$1,500–$5,000

	equipment (transportation not included)	
Dress shop	Six-month lease, inventory, utilities, phone, and advertising	$750,000
Beauty salon, personal care salon	Six-month lease, utilities, phone, and advertising	$30,000– $50,000
Restaurant	Six-month lease, utilities, phone, commercial kitchen, and equipment; liquor license and food department accreditation; china, silver, tables, and chairs; breakage; staff	$100,000– $500,000
Retail shop, larger scale	Fixtures, display units, cash register, inventory ($500,000)	$600,000
Manufacturer—picture frames	Machinery ($45,000), lumber and other materials such as wood and glass inventory, business cards, wood-working equipment ($160,000)	$205,000
Financial PR	Office furniture and equipment, phones, lease, insurance, legal fees (mostly to set up partnership agreement), stationery and business cards, secretary	$30,000
Karate school	Rented space, flyers, student agreement forms, application forms	$2,000
Software developer	Computer equipment and supplies, electricity fees, business cards	$40,000

Hidden Costs Can Kill You.

One of the greatest pitfalls you may encounter when you start up a company is discovering that you completely overlooked some costs.

Even a well-prepared, well-informed businesswoman can make that mistake. Chomie Persson, who owns a lawn equipment company in Little Silver, New Jersey, was totally unprepared for some taxes she incurred. Furthermore, she was surprised by the burden of paperwork, an additional cost factor many underestimate. "We came into it blindly," she recalls. Luckily Persson was able to absorb the cost and now operates a thriving undertaking.

Being surprised by hidden costs is not a function of stupidity or illiteracy. It happens to highly educated and sophisticated people who know a lot about a lot of things—except their own cost of doing business. Two experienced public relations experts were astonished by their expenses when they first opened shop. "The first thing our accountant asked us is whether we had insurance on our equipment (typewriters and office equipment). We said, 'What?' We were totally ignorant. Then he asked what would happen if someone stole it. We became paranoid about the risk. Insurance was a cost we had never considered. We knew we'd need medical insurance, but we never thought about liability insurance and equipment insurance."

Most often in a company you find another hidden cost is the wear and tear on yourself as you go the extra mile to stay in business.

For instance, entrepreneurs often underestimate the difficulty of getting clients. If you're a caterer, for instance, you may have difficulty persuading people to hire you. You know you're good, but they don't until you have a chance to show them. Getting that first foot in the door can be tough.

Comparisons of
Foolish Versus Intelligent Financial Risks

Foolish	Intelligent
1. Find a lucrative business and learn to love it.	Find something you love and learn to make it lucrative.
2. Invest your entire savings to launch a business that is new to you.	Work in a similar business first. Learn from someone else. Then start your own business cautiously.
3. Assume "What I like, others like." Listen to your friends.	Survey the marketplace carefully. Talk to people already in the business.
4. Assume that if your product is good, you can be in a foul mood when you feel like it.	A good product from a charming proprietor has a decided advantage.
5. Sell a product in one place that's being sold exactly the same across town.	When you sell the same product as someone else, add a personal touch or added service with it that individualizes your business.
6. Try to make a big killing fast.	Begin slowly. Grow as you know your market and your business.
7. Start with a full range of goods and services to have something for everybody.	Focus on a small market and expand it slowly.
8. Price goods cheaply, hoping you can raise prices as your products "catch on."	If it's a new product, such as smoked trout, give samples for customers to taste. Educate your customers about your price.
9. Charge cheap consulting fees because you don't know what the market will bear.	Find out what your competition charges. Price yourself accordingly.
10. Assume the merchandise you are selling will arrive as promised.	Assume deliveries of your inventories will be slow.

11. Assume your customers will pay promptly.

Assume some will "stiff you."

12. Charge different prices to different people.

Develop a price list. At most, have only two prices:
    a. corporate or bulk
    b. individual or single

13. Take as many orders for your goods or services as you can.

Be sure you can deliver before you promise.

14. Assume your goods or services will be the basis of your reputation.

Your own business practices will be the basis of your reputation.

15. Assume a mediocre reputation can be lived down.

A good business reputation is one of the greatest assets you can have in business.

16. When you're strapped for cash, pay your creditors on a first come, first served basis.

When you're strapped, explain to all of your creditors. Pay them equitably. Pay everyone back exactly as you promise.

17. Forgo goods or services you need but cannot afford.

Explain your situation. See if in exchange for future loyalty you can negotiate the terms.

18. When you begin to get successful, forget your old friends and associates.

Loyalty is a virtue. Should you fall into difficulties, it's your old friends and associates who will come to your aid.

19. Back a real "go-getter."

Never invest in a business you don't know.

20. When strapped for cash, look for a partner who can put up some money.

Choose a partner based on trust and compatibility of style and goals.

21. To finance a company, try to borrow as much from banks as possible and use as little of your own money as possible.

Banks are expensive. As a general rule, you should be able to put up a dollar of equity (from yourself or other investors) for each dollar you borrow.

22. When strapped for cash, threaten your customers and other creditors you will get a collection agency after them.

Offer special incentives to customers willing to pay up front quickly.

Terms to Use for Analyzing Your Financial Prospects

Fixed Costs—Ed Mendlowitz of Siegel, Mendlowitz & Rich, a New York City accounting firm, defines this as "costs that will occur whether or not there are sales or no matter what the sales volume." This is rent, your secretary if she is full-time, utilities, and the cost of your car if it is essential to your business. Even if no business crosses your door, you have fixed costs. You usually figure these on a yearly and monthly basis.

Variable Costs—These are costs you would not have incurred if you had not made a sale. If you have a sewing company, they represent the costs of the materials in a stuffed toy you sold. If you have a car dealership, they include the cost of the car and the commission to your salesperson.

Overhead—This is a more general way of talking about fixed costs. You need to price the goods or services you sell high enough to absorb the cost of your overhead.

Profit Margins—After you add up all your costs and subtract them from your sales, you have your profits. Profit margins are usually stated as a percentage. For instance, let's assume you have an art gallery and you want to figure out your margins for the month. Your sales were $10,000 and your overhead, figured on a yearly basis and divided by 12 (for one month's overhead), was $9,000. You have a profit margin of $1,000, or 10 percent of your revenues.

If your overhead had been $12,000, you wouldn't have had a profit. You would have shown a net loss of $2,000 for the month.

Return on Investment (ROI)—This refers to the money you make with the money you invest in your company, generally stated as a percentage figure. If you invest $10,000 to begin a consulting venture and you make $12,000 the first year, you've had a 20 percent return on your investment. (It is usually determined on a yearly basis.) The ROI figure acts as a thermometer for measuring the health of your enterprise.

Incidentally, many businesses do not realize a return on the initial investment for the first couple of years. Further, the size of your investment has little to do with the likelihood that you will recoup it. Success is determined by having the right business in the right market—and hard work.

Inventory Turnover—This is the length of time between your purchase of an item for sale and its actually moving off the shelf and out the front door. If you invest in an inventory of $50,000 for a boutique and six months later $45,000 of that inventory is still there, you have a problem. The faster you can move the inventory and "roll your money over," the more you can make.

The longer those items hang on your racks or sit on your shelves, the more concerns you may have. Is your product facing obsolescence? If it sits there long enough, will it become outmoded? Is your product perishable? If you have a flower shop and nobody buys your flowers, they die. Flowers have a very short "shelf life."

Cash Flow—The amount of cash you have in a company has to do with balancing your obligations (moneys due others) against your receivables (moneys due you). Your cash flow also may be based on the turnover of your inventory. Banks are very impressed by high cash flow. The amount of cash flow your company can generate will be a factor in the credit terms you are able to negotiate.

Cash Cow—This is a business that, with relatively small fixed costs, generates a great deal of cash flow. A travel agency can be a cash cow. With heavy volume a great deal of money passes through the coffers of the agency as the total fares for hotels and transportation are paid to it. A few days later the agency remits to the hotels and airlines, deducting the percentage to which it is entitled. Banks like cash cow businesses because they enhance a bank's own cash flow.

Capital—Cash. Money.

Initial Capital Requirements—This is the amount of money required to start up a business. It includes buying the desk and the typewriters and furnishing the office in a service business. It includes buying a showroom and stocking your initial inventory if you are opening a boat dealership.

Capital-Intensive—This refers to a company that requires relatively large amounts of money to buy equipment. Manufacturing businesses, if you buy the factories that produce, can be capital-intensive. The textile business, which relies on giant weaving and dyeing facilities, is capital-intensive. Service businesses are far less capital-intensive, since a service does not require a factory.

People-Intensive—This refers to a company where your major cash outlays go for bodies to staff the shop. A food franchise can be people-intensive, since you need a lot of teenagers to cook and package the hamburgers. A health camp can be people-intensive, as you provide exercise instructors, restaurant staff, room service, and maintenance and beauty care staffs. These businesses are also referred to as "labor-intensive."

Service Business—This is a business that provides a service rather than a hard product. Some service businesses are:

Real estate sales	Cleaning and maintenance
Public relations	Instruction
Production	Travel agency
Consulting	Beauty care
Moving services	Chartering, as in planes or boats
Secretarial services	Equipment repair and maintenance
Professional skills	Creative skills

Marketing—How you sell a product entails more than the sale itself. It also deals with how you advertise and the amount of exposure you are able to bring to your business. Whatever you do, be absolutely certain you know where your market is and how to reach it.

Bottom Line—This refers to the amount of profit you make after all your costs of doing business have been factored in. Once upon a time, on accounting sheets for businesses, the bottom line was where the net profit the company made was entered. Accounting forms changed, but "bottom line" retained its original meaning.

One-Time Expenditures—These are expenses you incur only once for major parts of your business. If you purchase the building where your company is housed, that's a one-time cost. The purchase of a new computer to run your real estate business is another one-time outlay. These are also called "nonrecurring" expenditures.

Synopsis

Terms to Use for Analyzing Your Financial Prospects

Fixed Costs—	Costs you are stuck with regardless of how business goes, such as rent, utilities, permanent staff.
Variable Costs—	Costs that vary as your business varies. The materials and commission you pay for the product you sell.
Overhead—	A more general way of talking about fixed costs.
Profit Margins—	How much money you are left with after all your costs have been tallied up.
Return on Investment (ROI)—	The amount of money you are able to make with the money you've invested in your business.
Inventory Turnover—	The rate at which your merchandise moves off the shelves. You want a rapid turnover.

Cash Flow—	The amount of money that comes into your company, then goes out.
Cash Cow—	A business that, once established, generates an unusually large cash flow.
Capital—	Cash.
Initial Capital Requirements—	The amount of money required to set up your business.
Capital-Intensive—	Describes a company that requires plant and heavy equipment, such as a manufacturing facility.
People-Intensive—	Describes a business that when operating requires an unusually large number of people to staff it.
Service Business—	A business that provides a service rather than a product.
Marketing—	Everything required to sell your product or service to the people you want to buy it. Good marketing is often the key factor in success.
Bottom Line—	How much profit (if any) you've made after all the costs are tallied up and subtracted from your total revenues.
One-Time Expenditures—	Expenses that only occur occasionally over years of doing business.

CHAPTER FIVE

How to Land Your First Bank Loan

Figure Out How Much Money You Need.

As a rule of thumb, you should be able to sustain your business for three to six months before you bring in $1 worth of income. Thus, if your estimated costs are $5,000 a month, you'd need $30,000 to $50,000 to start. Therefore, if you only have $5,000 to start, you'd do well to keep your operating costs down to less than $1,000 a month.

You Don't Want to Borrow Too Much.

As a general rule, you should be able to put up a dollar of equity (from yourself or other investors) for each dollar you borrow. You want to limit your debt because you have to pay interest on it. The lower you can hold your interest debt, the better off you are.

Watch every penny you spend for the first six to twelve months. Don't fall into the trap of trying to impress people before you've achieved a lot. Do not have more image than substance. Use cheap office furniture until you can afford a fashionable office. Follow the example of crackerjack Debbie Storrs, who started her collection agency out of her house with $5,000 until she had it on the move. Within a few short years she had over a $12 million-a-year business.

Few businesses can be started without money, even if all you need is $300 for sewing supplies or $5,000 to launch yourself as a consultant. By starting a service business you can avoid the costs associated with manufacturing, which requires equipment and materials, but even a service business takes money to begin. A restaurant requires kitchen equipment, a location to operate, and china, tables, employees, and advertising. A boutique requires a location and advertising, as well as its initial inventory of goods.

The first place you may think of going is a bank.

What Your Banker Wants.

Anita Miller, chairman of the recently founded AmeriFederal Savings Bank, advises, "Any woman going to a bank should do her homework. People don't realize that banks are really looking for business. Their employees may not always convey that. But a bank's business is not just taking deposits. It's making loans. But you've got to approach them with your facts, a solid pro forma, and a good business plan. Energy and enthusiasm are clearly not enough."

All your banker really wants is to be reassured about two things: that your company will be able to make a profit, and that you are the right person to run it.

Besides the cost and profit projects you have prepared to show your banker (as explained in chapter 9), you should not overlook another key ingredient in your business's success—customers. If you can convince your banker that your audience is there and that you can persuade potential customers to become real ones, you are more likely to win the vote of confidence resulting in your obtaining a loan.

The hardest thing to prove to your banker may be that you are the right person to run your undertaking. Here, the easiest way to demonstrate your capability is by pointing to your experience in a related area.

With the assistance of a friend, organize a resume summarizing your previous experience. Do not be modest. Make the most out of any experience or accomplishments that might impress someone. It is good to have a friend help, because often it is easier for your friend to dress your background up in the best light than it is for you to write a puff piece about yourself. Your track record may be a critical factor in your landing the loan.

Remember that bankers are an insecure breed. What they really want is enough reason to justify their having loaned you the money if you fail and are unable to repay the loan. They want something to point to on paper if worse comes to worst to show that they had good reason to lend you the money under the circumstances.

Look the Part.

Dress in a manner your banker can relate to. Invest in a dark "banker's suit" that you can wear for all your banking interviews. It should be dark, tailored, and look expensive. With this you should wear a high-necked tailored blouse. You don't want to look poor. You want to look as though you are already prosperous. Looking as though you are already successful has a positive psychological effect.

Even if your new enterprise is a lawn maintenance company and you would never wear a suit on the job, wear one to visit your banker. It makes you look serious and businesslike.

Put Yourself in the Banker's Seat.

Tell your banker what he or she wants to hear. Stress your experience, your reliability, your tenacity and skill. Show enthusiasm for the project. Focus on the positive aspects of the business, downplaying the negative ones.

Don't Delude Yourself.

Accept the fact that if you are beginning a new business, you will not be the bank's favored customer. Banks' favorite types of loans are not for new businesses. They much prefer to loan money to you *after* you are established.

Be Prepared to Shop Around for a Bank to Back You.

Look for a banker who will believe in you. Then be prepared to use collateral to get the loan. When Neuma Agins wanted to begin her own sweater business in New England, having been a design consultant in the knitting world for years, she had $25,000 in savings to invest and she wanted to raise another $50,000. "I went to the local bank. They wouldn't give me a loan. They looked at me only as a woman and asked questions like 'How long will you be doing this?' They just didn't have the vision. I was already employing twenty-five to thirty people, but partly the bank just didn't understand the garment business. So I took all my money to a New York bank and they gave it to me, but I had to risk everything. I had to sign my life away. I used the house and car as collateral. Then I really got scared. It was like being let down in a helium balloon in the middle of Las Vegas and finding that you had better gamble or you couldn't get out of the place." The gamble and risk were frightening, but, notes Agins, "It's also very exciting to finally invest everything in what I believe in—myself."

After you have a track record, the banks will love you. Neuma

Agins proved she knew what she was doing. That first year she showed a pretax profit of $40,000. Three years later, hiring two hundred people, she has a flourishing business with revenues of $2 million. Now that everything has turned out so well, bankers are her new best friends.

Don't Assume a Bigger Bank Will Be a Better Prospect.

Stay with a bank that already knows you. Patricia Duncanson, who with her husband owns Duncanson Electric Company, a Queens, New York–based contracting firm, was able to garner only $14,000 in company revenues during the first year of operation in 1977. But after the Duncansons landed a sizable contract with a large government agency and had to hire more employees, they went to a major New York City bank for a loan. "The bank wasn't interested," recalls Duncanson. "It was partly our fault, because when we started the business, we wanted a large, corporate, impressive 'business' bank. We switched our account from our local bank, and that was a mistake because the big-city bank wouldn't give us a loan when we needed it. So we tore up the checks, took the money from the account, and went back to the village bank we had been with at first." Finally, using their home as collateral, the Duncansons were able to get their loan. The firm took off after its first cash infusion. Duncanson Electric now bills over $3 million in sales and employs twenty-five to fifty full-time workers.

Sometimes you may even have difficulty just getting a bank to handle your business account. Relates Elizabeth Woolf of Renta Yenta, "Originally, no bank wanted to give us a loan or handle our business account. They don't like new businesses, risky businesses, run by women, not knowing if the account is going to exist or not. And we went to a few banks before we realized we had to go to one which knew us from the places we worked and using a man I worked for before as a reference. We could not walk into a bank cold and say, 'We are incorporating tomorrow and would like to open an account with you,' because right away they'd say, 'We're not interested.' Finally we went to a smaller, much more personal bank that knew me from my personal account before and the business account of the business I had worked for."

"I hate banks. I wish I could teach them something about the service business," declares a woman who heads a public relations firm. "They don't know what client service means."

Women Continue to Be Taken Less Seriously When They Confront the Male-Dominated Banking Structure.

If you feel that you are, shop around for a new banker. Debbie Storrs, who heads up a collection firm in Houston, had a hard time being taken seriously. She raised $5,000 to begin D. Storrs & Associates, using property as collateral. She subsequently felt the bank was discriminating against her and changed banks. "They had no idea little old Debbie Storrs would be doing $100,000 cash flow through the bank. Only it ended up not being that bank! I pulled my money out. I went out and shopped for a female loan officer who was aggressive and could understand my needs. I found one. Now she's changing jobs and I'm taking my business with her," continues Storrs.

Be Persistent.

Don't settle for a "no." No means many things. No can mean "no" or it can mean "we're not sure."

If you've been rejected by a bank, you're in excellent company. Some of the most successful women in our culture have been rejected. When Lillian Vernon Katz wanted to borrow some money initially to fund her mail-order business, which now has revenues over $135 million, she encountered resistance. She had to physically transport her AT&T stock certificates to her banker before he would accept them as collateral and give her the loan she needed. Even more recently, her bank refused to give her a loan to build a second building to house her burgeoning business. Katz didn't hesitate: she shopped around and quickly found another bank. She immediately severed all relationship with the previous bank. You can be assured they were sorry.

When Deborah Szekely wanted to borrow money to supplement $750,000 she had on hand from a property sale to fund the new Golden Door spa in Escondido, California, she shopped the local banks. "I was turned down by every bank in San Diego and some banks in Los Angeles," she recalls. "I wanted to build something grand, and the bankers didn't like a single-purpose facility." Szekely held out and found a bank to back her. She remains loyal to that bank until this day.

When you get the money from the banks, you get to spend it, of course. Having fought so hard to get the money, the sensation can be strange. A retail shop owner recalls, "I never really understood about using a bank's money. It unnerved me initially. I used to be apprehensive about spending their money." She systematically increased the size of her credit. She borrowed $25,000 initially and paid it back. Then she borrowed $40,000 and paid it back. Then $60,000, and so forth. She recently borrowed $110,000, and she's feeling very proud of herself.

If you can get money from a bank at a time when you also have savings, spend the bank's money first, observes accountant Nancy Rosenband. "Use your savings as a reserve in case you need it later, because the largest problem in new business is cash flow. Most people go from hand to mouth for a year or so no matter how much they start off with or what the business is."

Borrow Before You Quit Your Job.

If you want to start your own business and you have a job, you can borrow about 15 to 20 percent of your annual salary as an installment loan. Borrow it. Then quit. It would be a big mistake to try to borrow after you quit a job.

Some banks specialize in certain industries. So if you are going to set up a business in the same industry where you work, look at your paycheck, then call that bank and ask to speak with whoever is in charge of that industry.

Speak Your Banker's Language.

If you talk like your banker, you will most likely be taken more seriously. Learn the buzzwords to ring the bell of any banker.

Buzzwords for Bankers

Before you talk to a banker, arm yourself with the essential financial concepts they like to hear. Knowing the key words and using them comfortably make you appear businesslike and savvy.

Hard Assets—This refers to the property or tangible assets that you or your business hold. Usually hard assets are cash, stock and bond certificates, real estate holdings, work facilities, equipment, or inventory. Bankers really get excited when they see equipment. They used to get so excited about America's steel facilities, even though the plants were outmoded and uncompetitive, that the banks continued to bankroll the decrepit industry.

Good Will—This is something difficult to put a price tag on, since bankers prefer hard assets. Good will refers to the completely intangible advantage your business may have due to your popularity, a superior location, or the quality of your repeated patronage. It is worth a great deal to the success of a business. How much you can get your banker to admit it is worth is another matter.

Collateral—This refers to assets you might be forced to sign over to the banks as a sign of your good faith in maintaining your financial obligation and of your intentions to repay a debt or mortgage. When you make good your obligations, the full title of the assets reverts back to you. Typical collateral for starting a business might be your house, car, or money instruments you hold. If you are already in business, you may be able to use your facility, equipment, inventory, or even future receivables as collateral for a loan.

Debt Service—This relates to your interest payments and can include penalties assessed against you if you are late making a payment. Read the small print of your loan papers, particularly if you think you might be cash-strapped. Negotiate to keep the penalties to a minimum. If you think you're not going to have this problem, worry about the penalties anyway—sometimes unforeseen difficulties arise that force you to be overdue on a debt payment.

Revolving Credit—This is when a bank agrees to supply credit for a specified amount to you whenever you need it for whatever your needs may be. Whether or not you draw against the line of credit, the bank may charge you for holding it open. Revolving credit can be an expensive security blanket, since the fees, which are charged in addition to the normal interest rate, are often quite steep.

However, if you have a steady payroll to meet but your business is highly seasonal, revolving credit can see you through until the cash you expect flows back into the company. As soon as you receive payments from clients, you repay the bank. You can draw against your line of credit time after time, always repaying quickly after your unusual financial needs drop off.

To get revolving credit, you must have a track record and proof of the seasonality or fluctuations of your business. For instance, if you are an advertising agency, the contracts you have with clients to repay you for advertising space you filled are important to reassure your banker. A track record of previous payment by your clients provides further assurance.

Revolving credit has often proved to be an extremely helpful arrangement that can "make ends meet" when cash flow is erratic.

Credit Terms—You want the sweetest repayment terms possible with your suppliers. If you can stretch payments out to sixty or ninety days after you have received your supplies without being penalized, do it. If your creditors threaten you with penalties, cajole, beg, and plead on your hands and knees. But then pay when you promised, because when a creditor has been uncertain of your ability to pay and you come through, your believability is enhanced.

By lengthening your terms of credit with your supplier, you are able to keep more cash in the company till. Managing cash well is an important way to enhance your company's profitability. If you are able to keep excess cash on hand, you can invest it in high-yielding money market accounts for as little as a day at a time.

Prime Rate—This is the rate of interest you pay on money loaned by a bank if you are an established blue chip company. It is a standard to measure your loan against: it is the rate to which you ultimately aspire. When you first are granted loans for your company, you will probably be charged two or three points over prime. (A "point," in this instance, is a percentage point.) Since interest rates are already painfully high, you want to negotiate these percentage points down as low as you can.

Revenues—This is the total amount of money your company takes in. When you discuss revenues, you are saying nothing about costs. Revenues are not necessarily a measure of your success. It's profitability that counts. Huge revenues with even huger costs simply mean substantial losses.

Gross—This is short for gross revenues, the total money your company takes in before a single cost is deducted. Bankers usually don't use the term "gross revenues," preferring one word or the other instead.

Net—This generally refers to the net profit. "Net" means what is left over when all deductions have been made. Net profit is what you find on the proverbial bottom line.

Net is sometimes used as a verb: "I netted twenty grand last year," or, "I can net a good return on that."

Pretax and After-tax—This refers to your profits before and after taxes. If you are profitable and have little depreciation and tax benefits to take advantage of, your taxes may consume half your net profit. When you are considering the profitability of a venture, be sure to specify whether you are talking about pretax or after-tax profits. If the profits seem too splendid to believe, you're probably viewing them before taxes.

Life Insurance—Banks may want to insure you to make certain they are repaid any outstanding loans you owe in the event of your death. They routinely require you to take out an insurance policy on your life equal to the amount you owe them.

P&L—This is the way you should refer to your company's income statement, which in its simplest form deals with profits and losses. Talking about your "P&Ls" lends you an air of financial savvy. One suggestion: Don't just talk about your P&Ls. Get involved in the intricacies of the bookkeeping for your company. Know precisely how much profit you are making and where your prospects of increased profitability lie.

Targeted Market—Also called "market segment," this refers to the people you believe you can get to buy your goods or services. Only half of a company's success comes from its concept and ability to produce; the other essential part is getting the customers and clients you've targeted to find you. After they are aware of you, you must price your wares so they will find them appealing—and buy.

Synopsis

Buzzwords for Bankers

Hard Assets—	Property or tangible things you own. You can point at them and see them. Bankers love them.
Good Will—	Intangible advantages you have in your business. Its popularity, its proven track record, or high-quality repeat clientele.

Collateral—	Assets you are forced to sign over to a bank as proof of your intentions to pay your loans.
Debt Service—	Not only the interest but penalties you pay if you're late. Read the fine print.
Revolving Credit—	A set amount of credit the bank reserves for you as needed. It can be expensive. To get it you already need to be successful.
Credit Terms—	You want everybody to pay you promptly. You want to pay your creditors as slowly as you can.
Prime Rate—	This is the rate at which banks lend money to companies when the companies have bankers standing in line waiting for their business.
Revenues—	The total amount your company takes in.
Gross—	This stands for gross revenues, the total amount your company takes in.
Net—	This is how much of a profit you make.
Pretax and After-tax—	Your after-tax profit may be far less exciting than what you figured to earn before taxes.
Life Insurance—	Your banker may want it as loan insurance. If you die, he or she still gets paid.
P&L—	This refers to the bookkeeping pages that show whether your company is profitable overall.
Targeted Market—	Whether you have a restaurant or a toy store, you should know exactly who will buy your goods.

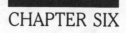

CHAPTER SIX

Other Sources of Money to Start Your Business

Friends or Venture Capital Can Be a Capital Idea.

More often than you might suspect, you can find friends who believe in your undertaking more than your banker. Once you've persuaded your friends to support you financially in exchange for a portion of the company, a bank is more likely to lend you the money. The reason: If your friends believe in you, they must know something the bank doesn't know.

Moreover, there are circumstances in which going to your friends can benefit both of you. If you have large inventory costs that you cannot fund out of cash on hand, instead of going to your banker and borrowing money at the current high rates, ask your friends to loan you the money at 10 percent. Ten percent is twice what some savings accounts pay and often above what money market instruments pay. Your friends may be happy to let you use their money for thirty or sixty days. This can be mutually beneficial: They earn higher interests than they normally would on their savings; you escape the top rates your bank would impose.

Your accountant or other advisor may help you connect with private individuals looking for new businesses to invest in. Remember however, that it is unethical for your accountant to receive brokerage fees from any transaction he is able to arrange. Most accountants will bring people together, then stay away from whatever arrangement is worked out.

If you are forming a new business and are willing to allocate parts of the business to others in exchange for financial backing, remember that the more successful you become, the more valuable the pieces of the pie will be and the more you'll want them back. One way to protect yourself is to arrange a buy-back contract at the outset. The contract should make it worthwhile for your friends to invest in you—at the same time it should protect you in case you're hugely successful. If you are, you can buy out your friends at a prearranged price, far less than the portion's real worth. Once again, the principle to keep in mind when you're inviting in private investors is that the best deals are those where both parties benefit.

If you are well connected in the business community, you may be able to find available venture capital for your company. People with venture capital often want a greater portion of your company than you are willing to give up. Once again, enter the transaction with a clearly stipulated contract that enables you to buy your partner out after you have built the company into a successful entity.

Small Business Administration Assistance.

The U. S. Small Business Administration is a federal agency created more than thirty years ago with about one hundred offices scattered throughout the country. You will find it listed under "U. S. Government Offices" in your phone book. The agency provides a number of services, one of which may be of particular interest to you as an entrepreneur. The SBA loans money directly to small business owners below the prevailing interest rates, and it lets you pay back the loan out of your profits over a long term. If this sounds great, it is.

However, there are two drawbacks. The first is that you already must have a good relationship with a banker. If a banker won't give you the time of day, your prospects with the SBA are bleak. The other, as you can well imagine, is that the competition for this kind of money is fierce, and the money is given out on a first come, first served basis. If you are in a hurry to get a company going, forget the SBA. The SBA is part of the world's largest bureaucracy, the U. S. government, and the wheels of progress there turn slowly.

For every businesswoman you meet who has received help from the SBA, you'll meet a hundred who have been turned down. Bettye Martin, chief executive officer of Gear, now a thriving company with retail sales in excess of $500 million in Gear-branded luggage, RTW, and coordinated household furnishings, says, "We tried the SBA. They didn't even want to talk with us. They said they had a lot of bad loans and they knew nothing about our business."

Venture Partnerships Can Be a Godsend.

If you have employed or know of a shrewd, canny accountant, you may be able to orchestrate a new kind of partnership that is far less onerous for you, the entrepreneur in need of cash, than a traditional one. It's technical and highly complicated and not something you should consider without top-notch accounting and legal advice, but it is a provocative arrangement to consider: you search out affluent investors who need tax write-offs and make them limited partners in your company. Almost all businesses have losses at first, and your wealthy investors are looking for losses to get tax breaks. Ed Mendlowitz of New York City's Siegel, Mendlowitz & Rich explains: "You distribute the losses according to what each investor contributes, but you don't have to give them the same percentage of the profits." Your wealthy investor is much happier to find tax losses than a little extra cash.

Then, when you break even, your partnership is already structured so that your limited partners receive only a certain percentage of the company after their loan has been repaid, or a certain return each year. There are many variables in venture partnerships, and the idea is worth considering. In essence, it provides you with interest-free cash for a relatively small price.

Your Own Savings Are Important.

More often than not, your own personal savings are your last resort. Whether they are $5,000 or $500,000, you are not alone if you are willing to reach into your reserves and fund yourself. However, you should tap your personal stash with great caution and some trepidation; putting your house and car up as collateral for a bank loan is the same thing as investing all your life savings.

Dianne Benson is an example of someone who launched her first wholly owned retail store with little caution and much trepidation. She sold her swank apartment and used the money to invest in the expansion of her own stores. She is successful today and has no regrets, but not everyone is so lucky, so take this step gingerly after you've thought through all other possibilities and the consequences.

Credit Cards Can Help.

You'd be surprised how many women with service businesses have financed themselves with their credit cards because they were the only borrowing available to them at the time. But this is the most expensive way to finance yourself, because most credit card companies charge at least 18 percent annual interest.

Persuade Your Suppliers to Help.

"I built my company on trade credit," says a woman who constructed a highly successful mail-order business. "I said to the printers, 'I promise. Please help'—and they did. I needed all the money I had for postage for the mailings." She succeeded and paid them all back. "Beginning that way keeps you humble," she adds.

When you're first starting out, negotiate lower rates for products and services you receive. This is one way you should negotiate it: "Charge me more when I can pay you more and I'll pay you. But right now give me a break."

Your attractive personality can be a big asset in cajoling your suppliers to extend you credit. Visit them in person and reassure them regularly. Make partial payments to show you haven't forgotten them.

Another way to reassure a creditor is to write a postdated check. If you expect to have money in fifteen days, postdate a check and ask the creditor to hold it for fifteen days; that way your creditor has something in hand.

In business—any business—your reputation is a very valuable asset. When you get behind in your payments to your creditors, be absolutely certain that you catch up—and keep your creditors informed of your situation.

"I've had some pretty dreary tough times, but I've never not paid back everyone I owed," explains a woman who struggled for years before she finally found a highly profitable proposition.

Make the Most of All the Money Your Business Has.

No matter what your company's financial situation, you should take advantage of some of the cash management programs many bankers offer. These programs allow you to maximize whatever money you have in hand. For instance, banks offer a lock-box system in which the bank takes checks as they come in during the day and clears them immediately, making the funds available to you instantly. This cuts out the expensive pastime of "waiting for the checks to clear." It also helps remove the possibility of overdrawing your account as you try to guess how many of your checks have cleared. Some of the cash management programs available also help you check the creditworthiness of your major customers, enabling you to hold up a shipment until the check is in hand and cleared. These and other cash management practices are going to be important aspects of future banking. Shop around. The bank that loans you money may not have the best cash management program.

Strategies
for Organizing
Your Business

CHAPTER SEVEN

Starting Off
Solo at Home

The Cheapest Way to Begin.

The easiest, cheapest way to begin a business is to supply your own skills and labor so you're not obligated to pay anybody else. Conducting business from your house can allow you to avoid spending money to lease office space. Moreover, if you work from your house, you don't have to pay for an additional telephone and desk. If you have children, you may be able to spare yourself the cost of a baby-sitter.

Starting off working at home is not the only way to launch a new venture, but it is an alternative you should consider before you begin.

Often It's the Best Way to Begin.

Sometimes women work at home only at the beginning, to minimize their costs until their business begins to grow. Such was the case of Debbie Storrs, who worked alone at her home for the first five months after she founded her collection agency. At first she did everything herself, from answering the phone to actually collecting the overdue bills for her clients. The business she began in 1980 for $5,000 in 1984 supported over twenty employees and boasted some $12 million in sales. Needless to say, it now also has separate offices.

Lynn Wilson, an architect who initially operated her design business from her Florida home, worked out of her den and car as she traveled to building sites when she was starting her company. "I kept brochures, stationery, and drafting plans in the trunk." Now Creative Environs is one of the most successful design firms in the country.

Even if you are a professional, you may have to start your practice working at home. Notes New York CPA Jill Feldman: "The first year was very hard. I didn't make any money for six months—it wasn't tax season. I spent the first six months building up business, making speeches, joining organizations, and getting my name known so by winter I had enough clients." As soon as she could afford it, Feldman moved into a separate office.

Some Businesses Make Long-Term Sense Being Based at Home.

There is not necessarily a conflict between business life and home life, and thus an office for some types of businesses may be completely unnecessary. Cheryl Hutto, an auctioneer of antiques, works out of her Stockbridge, Massachusetts, home. This gives her lots of space to store items for upcoming sales, and she is accessible around the clock, as many of the people she sells for are unable to see her until after five P.M.

There are times when operating your enterprise from your residence seems the logical thing to do, simply because the backup of an office is not essential. If you're good at working alone, it's only natural to conduct some business from your home—at least in the beginning. Your own backyard may be a natural place to begin a small day care center. If you are a television producer, you may rent studios to do much of your work and simply do the editing in your home—or use the facilities of the advertising agency that hired you. If you are a singer, you can practice at home because most of your work is done before an audience. If you are an appraiser, you generally appraise goods on site. If you are an interior decorator, you basically decorate other people's houses and may need only a desk at home to file swatches.

Some women who could easily afford an office and staff simply prefer to operate from their homes.

Mary Eileen O'Keefe, who heads a giant coal consortium, works from her antique-furnished home on New York's East Side and wouldn't have it any other way. "I love the freedom of working at six A.M. in my bathrobe. I'd hate to have to show up in the office every day," notes O'Keefe, who has worked from her residence for five years. O'Keefe is exceptionally disciplined, so she has no reason to consider moving to an office. Moreover, her job requires constant travel. Her office would sit idle much of the time.

If you are a creative person, working alone at home may be an important requirement of your work. Writers, designers, editors, composers, sculptors, and painters often strongly prefer to work at home. "The creative process is solitary," observes painter Denise Green. "You don't need anyone around to help you work."

How you view your home/office relationship can be a factor in how satisfactory you find working at home. Some entrepreneurs have purchased apartments primarily to accommodate their work. In effect, they "live at the office." Most of the space is used for their work, and only a minor portion of it is their living quarters. "I have a small home in a big office," explains media consultant Anne Ready in Los Angeles, who runs Ready for Media out of most of the rooms of her condominium. Artists and designers who work in large lofts often sleep in a bed in the corner.

How to Get Your Family to Take Your Business Seriously.

Once you've made the decision to work at home, how do you persuade your husband you are not out of your mind and that you are absolutely serious about starting this business? And how do you teach your children to respect your working time?

First, you really do need the support of your husband.

The easiest way to persuade your husband you are serious is to convince him that your new undertaking will be profitable and bring you satisfaction. Do your homework before you present the plan to him, so he can see that your idea is no passing fancy. Then keep a low profile until you achieve your first results. Once he sees that other people are taking you seriously, he'll be more inclined to do so.

It may take some time for you to train your husband not to rely on you too much to do home chores. One housewife who resumed a writing career at home after her children had grown up gave herself six months to gently teach her husband not to interrupt her during the day with as many as twenty phone calls. After she published her first big article she had his complete support and respect. He almost never interrupts her now.

Set up a working schedule and stick to it. If you are determined to work at home from nine to five, structure your traditional home duties as you would if you were going to work in an office.

If possible, designate a certain part of your living quarters as your working space and keep it off limits to general family use. Teach your children to answer the phone politely and how to take messages pertaining to your business.

If you have children, make sure they understand the difference between your working hours and the hours during which you are completely available. You'll have to train them not to intrude on your work time. If you decide to interrupt your work to tend to them, gently remind them it is an exception. Once your children see how much you enjoy your work and how serious you are, they will probably take pride in pitching in to help you by doing extra chores. A woman who sells real estate says that although she continues to put her family first, "Once I've got a hot deal cooking, the entire family makes it a priority. They back me up to the hilt." After a deal is closed she is careful to reward her children by taking extra time off to spend with them.

Set a realistic time frame for earning the respect of your husband and children for your venture, say six months or a year. Be persistent and demonstrate your determination. Don't be easily deterred. Once money begins to flow into the household from your efforts, you will find your "little undertaking" will gain some of the respect it deserves.

How to Have Other Business People Take You Seriously When You're Working at Home.

You may find when you start working out of your home that you are not being taken seriously. Comments a communications consultant who used to work at home: "At home I think you look like an amateur. If you have an office, you're no longer 'the free-lancer.' "

You don't have to move into an office to look professional, but you do need to go out of your way to communicate that you are absolutely serious.

You can begin this process by sending out notices to colleagues in your industry as well as to potential clients that you have decided to open your business. Send a press release to your local paper and trade papers announcing that you are commencing business.

Don't be chintzy about having business cards made up. Make them up by the thousands and give them out freely. If you are a magazine writer who left a job working at a specific magazine and you want to free-lance, your card should simply read "Jane Doe, Writer." If you are a free-lance television producer, your card should read "Jane Doe, Television Producer." "Free-lance" does not sound as professional. Describe yourself as "independent, working on projects for a variety of people." It means the same as free-lance, but it sounds better.

If you are going to use your home phone in your business, arrange for your family to answer it in a matter-of-fact, businesslike way. If the phone is an important part of your business, subscribe to an answering service to handle a phone number outside your home or buy a separate phone dedicated to your business. You don't want the conversations of your teenage kids interfering with a call from an important client.

You should have stationery printed up for correspondence and billing purposes. If you do not incorporate, simply print your name, address, and phone number at the top. Unless you want to make a statement, such as using fancy graphics to underscore the fact that you are a designer, stick to basic good-quality white bond paper with black lettering.

Don't be shy about billing. If you are undertaking a large project, arrange for payment in installments. In many types of businesses it is perfectly acceptable to expect payment on delivery. If your expenses are sizable, it is reasonable to ask for an advance to cover them.

Remember, you have a big commitment to yourself when you start up on your own. Once you've established your own business, you should be exceedingly reluctant to collapse it. If you don't take your own enterprise seriously, how can you expect anyone else to? You demonstrate you are serious by sticking with it. If you blithely walk away from one undertaking to begin yet another, not only will you have a more difficult time persuading your family to respect your next venture, but your customers and colleagues will find you less credible.

How to Signal You're Serious

Business Cards— No-nonsense and all business. Stay away from frills and flowers. Carry them with you everywhere. Give them out freely.

Answering Machine— Leave a businesslike message. Check in several times a day.

Answering Service— Have them answer the phone by identifying your company. Double-check

	them for accuracy. Check with them several times a day.
Telephone Manner—	Return your calls promptly. Be brisk and to the point. Have paper and pen in hand.
Home Telephone—	If you receive business calls at home, answer the phone by identifying yourself. Carefully instruct your family on businesslike phone manners. Keep a pad and pencil next to all phones.
Stationery—	Use no-nonsense and all-business stationery that identifies you and your business.
Briefcase—	Carry your papers in a briefcase when meeting with your banker, another business person, an investor, or anyone you want to impress.
Conversation—	Don't broadcast your problems. Talk about opportunities and recent successes.
Longevity—	Act as though you are in business to stay. The contacts you make today may not need you until next year. Make sure they know you'll be around.

Combating the Isolation.

There can be problems working at home all by yourself. "It's probably the hardest row to hoe," comments a psychologist. "The isolation can get you down."

Here are some pointers to help you work effectively when you run your business by yourself out of your home.

- Be up front when dealing with procrastination. You can get into trouble if you procrastinate.

- Take up a sports hobby or become a member of a gym. Find people in your social life who are unrelated to your work. Schedule breaks in your work.

- Get dressed for business whether you are going to your office or not before sitting down to work.

- Keep business hours. Since your clients keep business hours, they won't understand when you're still asleep at noon.

- Discourage your friends from calling you during business hours.

- Define objectives and set deadlines for yourself. Celebrate when you accomplish them.

- Don't let yourself get bogged down in minutia such as typing and running errands. For instance, don't waste half a day typing a letter when there are services that will type it for you for a reasonable fee. And don't deliver a package yourself when a messenger service would be just as effective. Keep yourself fresh for the most important aspects of your work.

- Go out of your way to make personal contact with the people you deal with. Seeing the face of the person on the other end of the phone can make your phone work less tedious.

- Don't form a partnership when you are depressed or feeling overwhelmed. Partnerships should be formed for other reasons (See chapter 9).

- Lunch with a colleague or client at least once a week.

- Entertain with cocktails or with coffee and dessert at least once a month.

- Go to seminars and workshops in your field. "It's one thing to have the support of my friends, but I need some from people in my field, too," notes auctioneer Cheryl Hutto, who works alone and at home.

There Are Tax Advantages to Working at Home.

If you want to deduct the part of your home you designate for business use, you should know that first you must set aside a sizable amount of space. Generally speaking, to get a tax deduction at least one entire room should be used for your business. It should have a desk in it and demonstrably be your business work area. For proof, in case the Internal Revenue Service disputes this, take pictures of it periodically, particularly when business is booming and it's chaotic, to demonstrate how the office in fact operates. In any case, you'll need a good accountant to determine how much you can deduct, based on the amount of time you work and the amount of space your work requires.

If you have a five-room apartment and you use one room for your full-time office, you could then pay a percentage of your rent with a company check. You would also pay a percentage of your electricity and heating with a company check. You might, if you have several electrical machines, be able to deduct a substantial part of your total electric bills.

The easiest way to deal with your telephone is to get a separate business phone and pay for it with a company check. Otherwise, it can get complicated; you have to mark off all business calls on your personal bill and be prepared to defend them to the IRS—again, if challenged. Keeping a phone log is the easiest way to do this.

If you are going to attempt any complex system of deductions, be sure you invest in a good accountant to advise you on how to set up your record keeping. Not only are the rules complex, but Uncle Sam changes them on a whim.

Do not be lax about your record keeping. The government is impressed by diligent documentation.

When Your Business Outgrows Your Home, You'll Be the First to Know.

The first indicator that it may be the time to move your business outside of your home will be money. Your company will be generating enough cash so that paying for another accommodation is a prospect you can afford to consider.

The next indication that you are ready to move is when your business begins pushing you out of your house. For instance, when you first open an antique restoration business, you may have room in your basement. When your business expands to the point that it spills into your dining room and kitchen, you should consider moving.

Usually the final weeks and months before you move your business into another facility are miserable, because once you make up your mind to move, it may be many months before you can find the proper space.

The owner of a thriving bakery discovered commercial kitchens were hard to find. But while she looked, her business continued to expand into her house. "We had sacks of flour piled up to the ceiling. I had moved in another oven for baking and we had bags of nuts everywhere. Mind you, this is the same kitchen where I had to make breakfast every morning for my husband and son. It was madness. We had to step over everything; while the ingredients were stacked up on one part of the house, the finished cakes were coming out the other side."

If the baker had begun to search for a kitchen six months before she needed it, she could have avoided some of the chaos and grief she encountered while her business thrived. If you have good indicators your business is outgrowing your house, don't put off looking for another facility to house it.

One note for your first move: Don't get excited and move into accommodations that are too large for you. Make conservative judgments and grow one step at a time.

Finding Your First Office Space.

The easiest way to determine space needs for your new business is to have first worked in your home until you have a good idea of what kind of facilities you need. While in your home you can get a feel for your space requirements and how much of it your business can sustain financially. Be realistic, after all, and don't expect to expand your little company into a giant undertaking overnight.

After you reach the point where you feel you should move out of your home, proceed cautiously. For instance, if you are in a business that requires a traditional office, before you commit yourself to setting one up from scratch, look around for someone in a related business who may have some additional office space that you can rent. Ideally this space will be furnished and you will also be able to share a receptionist and a secretary. Thus you can avoid making major financial commitments before your business has hit its stride.

The same technique applies if you have a craft or a service that requires specialized space. It is much safer to rent a corner of someone's studio or loft than to commit yourself to paying for the entire thing. Wait until you build up your clientele before you take a giant financial step.

The first location of your business ideally will be a short-term commitment, but long enough so you have an opportunity to gauge the success of your venture and time to see a steady income begin to flow into it. Only then should you commit yourself to the expense of running a full-time company.

You Can Always Go Home Again.

There is no ignominy in giving up an office and returning your business to your home. If the benefits of an office cannot justify its expense, let it go and work out of your home. This happens every day.

An image consultant explains: "I hired a little staff and got an office. But I like to keep my business small. Last year I planned to expand the business, but when I did a cost analysis, I realized I'd be getting more headaches but not more profits. So I went back to a home office. Besides, I basically do most of my work at my customers' homes anyway."

Elizabeth Woolf of Renta Yenta also moved back to her house. "When I had a partner we started in an office. But my partner left. Now I've moved my operation to my apartment. The prices of office space became so high, an office didn't make sense after she left. Why should I spend $1,000 a month on office space?"

Businesses That Can Be Conducted from Your Home

Antique dealing/restoration

Appraising

Art dealing

Art directing

Auctioneering

Baking

Bed and board

Catering

Ceramics

Child care center

Design

Editing

Film and TV production

Framing

House and lawn

Hypnotherapy

Interior decorating

Knitting

Management consulting

Medical consulting

Personal care

Photography

Psychotherapy

Public relations

Quilting

Sewing

Small appliance repair

Talent agency

Typing service

Writing

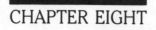

CHAPTER EIGHT

What Kind of Employees Should You Look For?

When you first start out you may be utterly without a support system. You make all your own phone calls, type your own invoices, and personally order your own stationery and supplies. At the same time, you are drumming up business and applying the special expertise to your enterprise that makes your business viable in the first place.

Who Should Be the First Employee You Hire?

The first person you hire will build the base of your entire support system. You need to find someone who helps take care of the details, leaving you free to ply your craft, whether it be engineering, sales, or decorating. You need someone who returns your calls with the messenger service or printer or stationer, leaving you more time to deal with existing clients or to solicit new ones.

The first person you hire must be very carefully chosen. Since you need someone to be charming, answer the phone, be flexible, and work almost as hard as you do, you may be tempted to make extraordinary promises to motivate a person to be all the things you need. Be sure to keep your promises conditional on the employee's demonstrated performance: if the employee fails, you do not want to be held to your initial promises.

You also need someone who can deal with the aspects of the business you dislike. Find someone who enjoys the things your business requires that you detest. If you hate numbers, hire someone who thrives on working with them. If you hate telephone contact, find someone who loves to talk on the phone. Don't belittle tasks you dislike: the person who performs them may find them challenging and satisfying.

Don't Try to Duplicate Yourself.

One of the most common mistakes neophyte entrepreneurs make is trying to hire someone just like them. It is important to recognize that the people who work for you are by definition different from you. They are not entrepreneurs. They work for someone—you. Their personalities will be different from yours. When you're interviewing, look for people you think will be able to do a specific job.

Different personalities lend themselves to different kinds of work. A quiet, timid person may be perfectly suited to being your bookkeeper and secretary. A flamboyant person may be your star salesperson and secretary.

You don't even have to like the people you hire, as long as you are compatible. But don't ignore "chemistry." Don't hire someone with whom your gut tells you you are going to have a personality clash. The smaller your business, the more important harmony among the various personalities becomes. The smaller your business, the more all your employees interact day in and day out and the more you rely on each of them to get their work accomplished.

Where to Find the Right Person.

Consider the customers and suppliers you already deal with who have employees who already know something about your field. There might be someone who already understands your business working out there who is looking for new "growth" opportunity—something you can provide.

Check with local schools and universities to find names of talented, hardworking graduates who may already be skilled in the areas you need. You might even phase a young student into your operation part-time while he or she finishes school, and later that person might join you full-time.

Place ads in local papers. Try to put yourself in the shoes of your ideal candidate when you write a personnel ad. Remember that while you do want to attract the person you need with your ad, you do not want to have hundreds of people who are totally unsuitable calling you. Be specific about what you are looking for.

Define the Job.

Take time to define carefully which aspects of the work you are most anxious to delegate and which ones are least important. Decide in advance the areas in which you are willing to compromise. It will only waste time if you interview a candidate who lacks the most essential skills the job requires.

Be honest about precisely what the job entails when you interview applicants. Do not promise the sky. Understand that the person you hire as your support system may find your work far less exciting than you do. Be realistic about the amount of growth and experience the candidate can find in your employ. Otherwise you may, in six months, find your employee frustrated and bitter.

Once You Find the Right Person, Use Him or Her.

Once you've hired someone, give him a job to do and let him do it. Give your employee the freedom to do the job, including the freedom to make mistakes, but watch closely enough so that when an employee slips up, you can step in quickly before the error grows large or costly. Try to use the mistake as a teaching experience.

If you are nervous about delegating, establish a reporting system where the employee continually keeps you updated on the progress of the project. Have the employee make a checklist of all the details of his or her work and review progress with you regularly. By staying closely informed it may be easier for you to adopt a "hands off" approach.

Once you have a person to take some of the burdens of your business off your hands, concentrate on doing what you do best. To be effective, you have to be fresh. To be dynamic, you need to be unfettered by nonessential tasks.

Don't Settle for Too Little.

Don't settle for someone who isn't "right." Use temporary help to fill in until you find the person you're looking for.

Whatever you do, don't fall in love with employees before you see them perform. Adopt a we'll-see-how-it-goes attitude when they first come to work for you. If an employee isn't working to your expectations, fire him or her without hesitation. The sooner you fire the person, the easier it is to hire another of the applicants you interviewed, reducing your time and aggravation.

Part-time Workers Can Be a Full-Time Solution.

Instead of looking for a full-time person, you may opt for one or more part-timers. If you can't find the assistant you want, two part-time employees might fit the bill. Kate McGrath of KM Media Productions in New York hired two part-time women to provide her support system. "They have different skills and work different hours." She finds the arrangement ideal.

Because of other commitments in their lives, highly qualified people may be available to work part-time who would never be available full-time. Housewives and mothers, college students, struggling musicians and actors are examples of the kinds of people who are often available to work part-time.

Thus a caterer can operate without a single full-time employee, bringing together additional people she has trained as cooks and servers to back her up as needed. A public relations consultant hires independent writers and graphic designers as projects come in, using only a part-time secretary to provide her with an administrative support system.

Hiring part-time workers can have important advantages. As a part-time employer you are able to avoid many of the responsibilities incurred when you hire people full-time. Depending on the frequency with which you rely on part-timers and the amount of time they work for you, you may be able to enjoy considerable savings. You may also be able to avoid substantial aggravation and paperwork.

Hire a Computer Instead.

Before you rush out and hire someone to back you up in your business, investigate the extent to which computers can help you instead. Computers can help you expand your own personal productivity.

For instance, state-of-the-art telecommunications units have a great little device called the automatic phone dialer, which can dial frequently called numbers at the press of a button. Press another button and the unit will redial "busy" lines as needed.

Typewriters with memories make it easier for you to handle your own correspondence. When you are pricing these machines, however, make tough cost comparisons between a secretary and a new electronic typewriter. It is easy to be entranced by new gadgetry.

Computers can be a godsend in the real estate business, where sophisticated interest and mortgage calculations can be brought to the screen merely by tapping a couple of keys. Small copiers can provide you with needed records while reducing your correspondence requirements—you can write a note on a letter and return a copy of it to the sender.

The extent to which a business should be computerized varies. Computers can be invaluable for bookkeeping and inventory control. They can be useful for cataloging contacts and key suppliers. Videotape players can provide clients with a "feel" for houses you may have decorated or events you have orchestrated.

On the other hand, you may have a business for which pertinent software has not been written. Don't buy a computer before you have a clear understanding of precisely how much it can help *you*.

CHAPTER NINE

Should You Have a Partner?

The idea of having a partner in your business can be very appealing. It means having someone around to rely on and to back you up. It means having another person to bounce ideas off of. It means you can be a member of a team, pulling together mutually toward the same goal, prospering together.

It sounds great. But look again. Almost anyone you ask who has ever had a good partnership has had several that were disasters. Indeed, there are no more vitriolic aftermaths in failed marriages than there are in some failed partnerships. People become disappointed, disenchanted, and disheartened when they see partnerships happily entered into become major miseries in their lives.

Do Partnerships Work?

Having a partner may sound like a marvelous idea, but far more fail than work. In fact, it is so difficult to form a viable partnership that you should make every effort to make it on your own without one. For almost everyone, a partnership should be a last resort.

Most people form partnerships because they want to expand the business or are insecure about making decisions alone. Granted, it is reassuring to have another intelligent person to help you succeed. But you are far wiser to form a loose alliance with someone in a related field (described in the following chapter) than to rush into a partnership.

The worst partnerships are the ones between friends. Your expectations are high and you think you understand each other. Wrong. Usually the partnership fails and the friendship goes with it.

If you have absolutely no other recourse but to find a partner, look among colleagues with whom you have successfully worked before and whose performance to date has been stellar. If you harbor any doubts whatsoever about the union, don't make it.

Moreover, should you decide to take a partner, keep your expectations low. The odds are your relationship will underperform even low expectations.

How Do You Find the Right Partner?

You find the right partner with great difficulty. It also takes patience, time, and a little luck. The secret of a successful partnership is to find someone with complementary skills, complementary work habits, complementary personalities, and complementary objectives.

Complementary Skills

Ideally, you should be strong where your partner is weak. If you are a marketer, you might team up with a designer and a financially oriented person, as did Bettye Martin. Assisted by complementary partners, marketer Martin has built a home furnishings company that licensed about $500 million worth of goods last year.

Once you find someone with complementary skills, you and your partner must trust each other and leave each other free to pursue separate areas of expertise without second-guessing each other all of the time.

The best partnerships have carefully defined roles for each of the partners, roles that do not overlap.

The same rules that assure you a successful partnership with another person also apply to a business partnership with your husband. Almost every successful husband/wife partnership operates by these rules. For instance, Adora Ku runs a software design firm with her husband. She is the administrator and marketer. He designs the software. Pat Cloherty, who heads up a New York investment banking and venture capital firm with her husband, says, "We have different backgrounds and specializations. His background is corporate finance and reorganization in addition to ventures, and I have always specialized in ventures."

Complementary Work Habits

You should investigate the work habits of the person you are considering for a partner. You don't want a partner who works six hours a day while you work twelve and who then expects to split the profits fifty-fifty. You don't want someone who spends three months at a time on vacation while you toil twelve months a year. By the same token, if your own family and marital responsibilities require you to work curtailed hours, you want to discuss this with a partner before joining forces. You don't want someone continually nagging when you are required to be absent from your business.

When you are considering someone to be your partner, talk precisely about what each of you means by "hard work." You must clearly define vacations. You should also, in advance, agree on a plan of action should either of you become seriously ill or otherwise disabled.

You should discuss day-to-day business management, agreeing

on how you would deal with cash binds and precisely how much each of you expects to be able to be paid out of the business.

Further, you should agree about the possibility of bringing family members into the business.

Your upfront discussions with a potential partner are time-consuming, but this is time vitally well spent. Just as in marriage, if you choose the wrong partner, the time you lose will be far greater.

Complementary Personalities

Getting along well together can make a tremendous difference in a partnership's survival. Understand that when you build a business you are exposed to all kinds of stress that will bring out the worst in everyone involved.

Chances are you and your partner will end up spending twelve-hour days together while you get your company on its feet. If possible, you should observe each other conducting business to see if your styles are compatible. If you are low-key and soft-spoken, will you be comfortable with a screamer? If you dress in a business suit for your work, will you be comfortable with someone who prefers blue jeans and works best playing rock music on the radio?

Complementary Objectives

Moreover, you should investigate the compatibility of your approaches to problem solving. If you encounter difficulties, will you agree about whether to hang in or go bankrupt? Does your potential partner share your philosophy of client service? You do not want to enter a relationship where you are continually having to apologize for your partner's behavior.

You should agree about the size of business you want to build and about your sales and marketing style and philosophy.

How to Avoid Picking the Wrong Partner.

No matter how desperate your financial situation, do not bring in a partner solely for money unless it is absolutely your final recourse. Unless you can pick a partner for the right reasons, the relationship has small chance of surviving.

Do not bring in a partner simply to expand your business. When you think about expansion, think about maximizing yourself and hiring good people to back you up. If you want to broaden the size of your firm, find good outside consultants you can contract with to help you offer expanded services.

Look at a potential partner's track record before you even consider entering into a relationship with him or her. Make sure the person can do what he or she promises.

When you are searching for your partner, do not take people at their word when they speak of their goals and ambitions. Many will simply mouth words that seem appropriate at the time. Ask yourself, "Is this person in touch with himself? Is this person likely to sing a different tune after six months of hardship, should the business run into difficulties?" Once again, a proven track record is the best testament to a person's drive, tenacity, and talent.

Investigate the potential partner's personal inclinations and lifestyle before you enter into a partnership. They can interfere with business. A woman joined forces with a man in a food business, convinced that her expertise in the kitchen and his selling abilities made a great fit. She failed to check his personal life, which ultimately destroyed the partnership. For one thing, her partner had a violent love life. He and his lover routinely beat each other up. "He and his lover were disabled from a brawl the night before we had a party for 2,200 people," she says. "Moreover, he had a drug problem. Money was always disappearing."

Does It Matter If Your Partner Is Male or Female?

Whether you team up with a man or woman depends solely on your needs and personal inclinations. Finding someone with whom you are compatible is far more important than the gender of the partner you ultimately choose.

Since women are often still discriminated against in the business world, a man can prove an asset: it's not a pleasant thought, but it is true. Lynn Morgenroth, who is in a business partnership with David Walke, in financial public relations, says, "It turned out to be good that he was a man. This is a very personal service business and there are clients that work better with a man at first until they get used to me."

Some women have deliberately opted for male partners because they feel a male viewpoint helps temper or balance their own outlook.

You Should Draw Up a Contract.

Once you think you have found the right person and you feel certain a partnership is going to work for you, the first thing you should do is draw up a contract.

The most important thing you should consider is how to get out of the partnership should it fail. Most partnerships do. Most partnerships begin filled with goodwill and trust and terminate with hostility and ill will.

"You've got to write the partnership agreement while you're still talking to each other," advises attorney Marcia Goldstein. You have to assume that when the partnership dissolves you won't be on speaking terms. Most partnerships are like ill-fated marriages: write the contract as you would the prenuptial agreement.

The contract should spell out a formula for buying each other out or for selling the business to someone else. It should spell out what would happen if one of you should get sick or have a severe disability. It might even cover what would happen should one of you experience a breakdown. A contract may also cover day-to-day things such as who signs the checks.

Your contract should protect you, your beneficiaries, and your business. It should protect your investment in the business and define precisely how the costs and profits are to be shared.

Lawyers can help with your contract, but they frequently decline to advise you specifically about what to include. Before you undertake a partnership talk to other people in related businesses who have solid long-term partnerships to get their suggestions on what your contract should include. Be careful to tailor it to accommodate any of the unique circumstances your business may include.

Do not take your contract lightly. It is your best insurance against an unhappy, inequitable end to your partnership.

Advantages of a Partnership

You have another person to work on the business. Your partnership can provide you with more flexibility in scheduling or tending to your clients.

Your partner adds a needed skill.

You have someone to communicate with about the business. You are not alone.

There is greater growth potential.

Your partner brings new business to the company.

Your partner may bring money to the venture.

Your partner may be strong where you are weak.

Your partner may like to do the things you dislike doing, and vice versa.

Ingredients of Successful Partnerships

Separate responsibilities.

Clear-cut responsibilities.

Partner selected after extensive interviews of other candidates.

Different skills.

Complementary personalities.

Ability to enjoy sharing work.
Constant communication.
Ability to share credit with partner.
Ability to share responsibility for failures.
Shared goals for the undertaking.
Sharing is valued.
Both parties prosper.
Sense of humor: laughter is the best medicine.

Disadvantages of a Partnership
You are restricted in changing the direction of the business.
There is reduced flexibility in your work load.
Someone is always looking over your shoulder.
You have to share the profits.
There are limitations on your putting family members on the pay-roll.
There are limitations as to how much money you can take out of the company and the salary you pay yourself.
There is less money for you.
There is less flexibility in the location of the business.
There is a lot of tension and friction during tough times.
If the company fails, your partner may blame you.
If the company succeeds, your partner may take the credit.

The Most Common Reasons Partnerships Fail
Partner brought in solely to raise money.
Partner brought in solely to perform one service and performs unsatisfactorily.
Overlapping responsibilities.
Different concept of company's direction.
Different concepts about money being spent.
One person feels she or he is doing all the work.
One person goofs off.
Personality clashes.
Different life or management styles.
Different philosophies of how business should be run.

The Most Common Reasons Partnerships Fail (continued)

Different ambitions.

Unwillingness to share credit.

Competition between the partners: ego clashes.

Disagreements over money being spent.

Disagreements over rate of growth.

Disagreements over direction of growth.

Greed.

One partner shifts priorities and goals.

One partner loses ambition.

Spouse conflict: interfering relatives.

Difficulties in the business: partners blame each other.

One partner feels the other hinders the company's progress.

One partner fails to produce as promised.

People's tolerance of change is different.

People change.

CHAPTER TEN

How to Form a Loose Partnership

You have another alternative to the solitude of the lone entrepreneurial practitioner and the responsibility of entering into a formal partnership: it is a quasi partnership, working in tandem with one or more people.

Tandem associations are relationships born purely of mutual convenience. In quasi partnerships you join forces on a limited basis to achieve separate but unconflicting goals. Each of you remains essentially an independent entrepreneur, free to chart the course of your business without the interference—or free advice—of the other.

Working in Tandem Succeeds for Professionals.

At its simplest, a tandem relationship consists of two professionals supplying complementary skills. Both careers are enhanced by the association. Such is the case with Pam Fletcher-Hafemann, who works in tandem with a plastic surgeon in San Diego, California, on a part-time basis. She is the director of a prestigious beauty program at a nearby spa and an expert on hair and makeup. Two days a month she books up to ten consultations a day at the doctor's office with his plastic surgery patients. His patients benefit from her presence, because after they have had a face lift they can also get updated makeup advice.

Fletcher-Hafemann also counsels patients on their hair design and color. "If a woman changes the color of her hair and looks well rested when she returns to her office after a face lift, the surgery won't be so obvious. Instead they'll think a woman looks great and focus on the new color or style of her hair."

Tandem relationships can involve larger commmitments, such as sharing a lease. Ruthellen L. Holtz, a lawyer in Columbia, Maryland, works in tandem with an accountant. They share an office. Holtz and her associate have separate secretaries and separate computers, but they share a reception area, a photocopy machine, and a direct line that goes into Washington, D.C. "We refer clients back and forth," explains Holtz. They also trade information.

Even Working in Tandem Can Require a Contract.

Even if the association you plan in your partnership is informal, you still should draw up an agreement. A written agreement should clearly define the specifics: who will pay for what and how those decisions will be made. For instance, if you are going to lease a copier, you will want to have the right to disagree if your tandem associate wants a fancy expensive one when all you need is something simple. The agreement should specify what percentage you would pay of equipment that exceeds your needs.

Further, you should have a written agreement, in addition to the lease, on how you will share the rent. You should specify the percent each of you will pay and one should indemnify and hold the other harmless. That way if one does not pay, the landlord only goes after the culprit. Finally, your agreement should delineate your obligations toward furnishings for the reception room, redecorating, and painting.

Even Loose Relationships Can Run Amok.

The hardest aspect to cover in an agreement to work in tandem with someone is the professionalism that you expect from each other. The best insurance is to get to know someone before you leap into a tandem agreement. For instance, you should have styles of doing business that are compatible. If your tandem mate routinely brings her barking lapdog or cranky children to the office, you may object. Moreover, if you refer clients to each other and one of you is slack about returning calls, the referrer looks less professional.

The Quasi Cooperative Provides a Network for Specialists.

A group of people in business can form a completely informal working relationship where all benefit by helping each other market products, refer customers, and complete major projects. This relationship is ideal for people who work in related, highly specialized areas. For instance, Rustin Levenson, who after eleven years as a museum painting conservator, is now working privately, "sort of in tandem" with seven part-time subcontractors, each a specialist in a different aspect of art restoration. Each has a different kind of expertise. "The thing that's cooperative is that we share a lot of information. We work out solutions to problems together, review things once a week to troubleshoot problems in the studio together. But it's very informal."

A quasi cooperative is an ideal arrangement for any group with highly specialized but related interests. Perhaps one person can even provide space for the others while working on different aspects of a shared project. Sometimes it is possible to take out group insurance together. Equipment, books, a computer, and different information can be shared to the benefit of all. Most important, you can refer clients to each other. No one has to participate except at will, and no one gives up any part of his or her identity.

Quasi cooperatives are best if you work independently or are starting a small business. If you have a larger or more established business, you may choose to go it alone.

Strategies for Buying Instead of Starting from Scratch

CHAPTER ELEVEN

Should You Buy an Already Existing Business?

If you are fortunate enough to have substantial financial resources, you have the option of buying a company that is already in business rather than starting one from scratch.

There Are Advantages to Buying a Preexisting Company.

The easiest way to be successful is to buy a company that has been in existence for at least a year or two. That way you bypass the trickiest part of becoming entrepreneurial—the early years. The great majority of businesses fail early in their existence.

There are numerous advantages to buying an already thriving enterprise. Foremost is that if you are faint of heart and do not feel you could handle all the start-up pressures, buying a preexisting company, where many of those decisions have already been made for you, will be ideal.

The fact that the business is already in existence is evidence that you won't have to lose sleep agonizing over the decisions the company's founder made. For instance, you don't have to pick a location—the business already has one that has proved viable. The inventory and equipment are already ordered and installed. Supplier networks have been established. Moreover, you have a history of inventory turnover to guide you in your sales projections and in placing future orders. Further, the business has already found its niche in the marketplace. It has an established clientele who have worked it into their shopping patterns. They already know what the business does and what products are offered.

If the company you buy has survived its initial growing pains, it has already proved it is a viable concept, and this viability gives you a tremendous advantage when you are talking to bankers. Some who wouldn't have given you the time of day as an entrepreneur in a start-up situation may be very willing to help you now that the toughest period of the business has been hurdled.

When It Makes Sense to Buy a Business.

Buying a preexisting business is a logical alternative if you want to relocate to an area where you find no suitable employer. For instance, if moving to Little Rock is the answer to your prayers, but there is no job for you there, you may opt to buy a restaurant or a retail shop and run it yourself.

If you dislike your life-style, buying a company can provide you with a dramatic change. Observes veteran business broker, Tom West, whose Business Brokerage Press puts out a newsletter for other brokers, "The main reason people buy a business is to get out on their own. People don't really buy a business for the money. They do it to get out of the rat race."

If you have already developed exceptional management skills, you can buy a failing business and turn it into a profit center. But this is a risky proposition recommended only if you have had previous successes running other companies and can design and put into action a solution. This is not something you should try unless you are a thoroughly seasoned businesswoman.

Drawbacks to Buying a Business.

The major disadvantage to buying a business someone else has founded is that it can never be completely your own invention. "I would never have been happy with a business I had purchased. It's the creation of something that satisfies me," says Deborah Szekely of the Golden Door and Rancho La Puerta.

"How could it be a personal reflection of me if I bought somebody else's idea?" wonders designer/retailer Dianne Benson.

If you buy a business, you should know that it will probably never be a completely hand-tailored reflection of yourself. A preexisiting business already has a life and character of its own, and that life was breathed into it by somebody else. It may have style and a pace different from yours. Moreover, the inventory and equipment may not be precisely what you would have chosen had you been in charge. If you buy a business, it may have characteristics that are not particularly pleasing to you personally. But you will have to live with these characteristics until you've made enough money to alter or replace them.

Maybe your purchased business is just about perfect, but the location is wrong in your estimation. Then you must decide whether to remain in a less than optimal place or move and risk losing the company's preestablished clientele.

Does Buying a Company Give You as Much Freedom as You Expect?

Not necessarily.

The business you are considering purchasing may be more work and a greater source of headaches than at first it seems. "When you buy an existing business you arc usually buying trouble," says

Edith Hamilton, who has built and sold several beauty salons over the past forty-five years. "If the company had a bad reputation, you have to rebuild it. If it had a good one, but the employees want to leave, you still have to rebuild it."

Enticing existing employees to stay on at a company after you become the new owner may mean that you end up essentially working for them. Since your personality is different from the previous owner's, it may take a profound effort on your part to motivate employees who were much fonder of their previous boss than they are of you. Advises Richard Rodnick, chairman of Geneva Companies, a middle-market investment banking firm, "You should ask yourself, 'If my personality is injected and the owner's is removed, will it work?' Do you know the people you're getting involved with, and can you see yourself managing them? It's naive to think that you can simply walk in and sit with your feet up on the desk and your employees will jump to their feet when you arrive."

If you have financial partners in your undertaking, your freedom can be even more sharply curtailed while your partners look over your shoulder and second-guess you. That can frustrate you if your primary reason for buying a business was to be your own boss.

"If you have to borrow one-third from your brother and one-third from a friend, you don't really own it anymore," notes Tom West. If you wind up with only one-third, you have in effect two bosses—the people you borrowed the money from. Thus, if your intention was to buy a business to be independent of everybody, you have not achieved this goal until you have bought all of the company.

When you decide to buy a business, be candid about your expectations of freedom and independence, and realistic about your chances to achieve these expectations in the situation you're considering.

What to Look for in a Business.

When you are investigating a company for possible purchase, you should look at that company's total picture. You should look not just at the company's drapes, typewriters, and products, you should also examine its clientele and reputation. You should investigate its relationship with suppliers to see if you are going to have to spend your time reassuring and coaxing vendors who have been stung by the previous management.

Try to imagine you are already running the business and figure out all the ways that things could go wrong.

It's not easy to find out what the net profit of a business is. Sometimes the sellers themselves are mistaken about what their profits are, and it may be your responsibility to figure out where the profits of a business lie.

Part of your investigation should center on the sellers themselves. How long have they been in business? What is their background? How long has the business been in existence? What is their reputation in the community? Why do the owners want to sell? Examine their reasons to see if they have been truthful with you.

And don't be dazzled by a business that is doing well but is only part of a fad. "Just because something's hot doesn't mean it's a long-term, viable business. You see all these software stores and all the health studios popping up and making a mint. But how long do you think they'll be around?" asks broker Tom West.

On the other hand, if a business is doing poorly, do not assume that you will be able to turn it around after buying it cheaply. For one thing, you cannot trust the advice of the owner as to the extent of the problems. If he or she is so wise, why did the business go so far afield in the first place?

One last detail you should check if you are serious about buying a business is whether the state and local operating certificates, operators' licenses, and the like are transferrable. If they are not, you should investigate the possible delays and difficulties you might have in obtaining authorization to continue the business.

Should You Get a Broker?

Whether or not getting a broker makes sense depends on your circumstances and your relationship to the company you want to buy. For instance, it would have been silly for Myrtle Willey to use a broker when she bought T. W. Dick, a steel fabricating company. Willey had moved up through the ranks in the business from secretary to president when she decided to acquire the company, and she already knew it better than anyone. "I didn't use a broker. I went to the banker I'd been with for years who knew my track record. The same was true of the accountant and attorney. So I had no problems putting a package together."

Willey's circumstances were unusual. But even if you have had long contact with a company as a supplier or customer, you can develop a feel for its operation and you can probably complete the transaction without having to pay—usually roughly 12 percent of the deal—a business broker.

There are circumstances under which you might opt for a broker even if you already know what business you want to buy, as did Cynthia Tabbert, who bought the Canary Cafe in Indianapolis. "I spent a year looking at many restaurants, but I had my eye on this one," she recalls. Tabbert used a broker anyway. She let him do much of the legwork. Her broker did a lot of the homework, checking taxes, titles, zoning, parking, and signs, some of which required investigating city correspondence back several years. In her case, a broker was a good idea because he did much troublesome work for her and earned his fee.

If you do not already have your eye on a business you want to buy, and you want to search for one, a broker can be invaluable. For one thing, a reputable business broker may have already analyzed the financial records of businesses, in order to get an idea of what the company's true profitability is. They are accustomed to sifting through the paperwork of company books and have experience that can be extremely useful to you—they are used to sorting out shoe boxes full of records and putting together an accurate picture of the company's financial history. Some brokers offer you a complete purchase package with all the taxes and legal ramifications worked out.

As do realtors, brokers act as middlemen between the buyer and seller, but because they profit when the deal is completed, they have a vested interest in finishing the sale. Brokers can be of great service to you, but be sure not to let them do your thinking for you. They can be a valuable resource, but never forget that they are working *for a commission.* Just as a real estate broker shows you the best features of a house and may not mention the fact that the basement floods every year, a business broker may be unwilling to tell you all the bad news about a company. There is never any substitute for doing your *own* homework. Even with a broker, most of the work is up to you. Be thorough and persistent in your investigation. You want to know any and all of the bad news *before* you buy.

Check a Company's Finances Before You Buy.

Often, particularly in smaller businesses, the profit and loss statement may not be an accurate reflection of the true profitability of a business.

A company can be far more profitable than it seems at first glance. Frequently, owners of businesses offer numerous perks and benefits to themselves and family employees. It is possible that several hundred thousand dollars may be spent each year on automobiles, household and personal helpers, vacations, and personal telephone bills. The records a seller shows you may have been prepared to satisfy Uncle Sam, not to show the business's true worth. It may take intensive investigation on your part to figure this out. You should examine all the bills paid by the company, as well as its bank record, to get an accurate view of the business.

By the same token, a company's debt can be greater than it seems. When you buy a company you must also be prepared to assume its past financial encumbrances. A company's existing financial obligations should be reflected in its ultimate sale price.

For instance, repaying a $50,000 bank loan the company took out the previous year becomes your responsibility once you buy the business: you deduct that from the price of the company. "Sometimes sellers will guarantee there will be no encumbrances as of the sales date," observes business broker David Goldfarb. "But that's impossible. Even when they do their best to clean them up, bills will come in after you've bought it. Who is obliged to pay them?" It could be you, the buyer. Be sure you address these matters *before* you buy the business.

If you have a broker, part of your contract may specify that he or she is responsible for sorting out all the pending bills a company has. If they miss a bill, *they* pay—not you.

You can simplify the possibility of future legal tangles with the seller by writing an arbitration provision in the sales agreement that covers problems that might arise in the future. This provision states that you and the seller agree that any future disputes will be handled by independent arbitration. Moreover, you both waive all right of appeal. "The lawyers hate this," says Goldfarb. They hate it because it reduces the possibilities of fees from prolonged lawsuits.

How Much Should You Pay for a Business?

The price of a company is determined in any number of ways, but the net result is that you should pay from three to ten times its true annual profitability. For instance, you can take the combined worth of the fixtures, inventory, and facility improvements and add one year's profits to give you a ballpark figure.

There are many factors affecting the purchase price of a company:

How fast the company has grown
What its future prospects for growth appear to be
The nature of the industry it is in:
    Is its industry thriving?
    How intense is the competition?

Whether rapid obsolescence is a factor in its future
Its financial stability and its hard assets
How much the company makes
Good will

Needless to say, if the company is in an industry with skyrocketing profits, projects excellent long-term prospects, has far outpaced the competition, makes a lot of money, enjoys a great reputation, and is financially stable, it will sell for a very high earnings multiple.

Good will is the most nebulous asset, since it is intangible. How much it is worth varies. If you are buying a restaurant that is a landmark institution with hordes of loyal, regular customers, its good will is worth a great deal.

Once a price has been asked, take it as a starting point and begin to negotiate downward with the owner. Negotiating the price of a company can be very intense if both seller and buyer are genuinely anxious to make a deal. Since most small businesses are seller-financed—you make only a down payment and the seller lets you repay the remainder over several years—there are myriad variables to iron out. If you can convince the seller that you have what it takes to make the business prosper, assuring profits from which to repay the rest of the price, you are likely to get a more favorable deal.

Should You Keep the Name of a Business When You Buy It?

If the company is successful, you should keep the name. If it is not successful, change it. If it is successful, you don't want to make customers uneasy. Don't let your ego prompt you to change it. If you're transforming the business, then by all means change the name. Tom West says he has witnessed serious mistakes: "I've seen Chinese people buy a pizza place, change it to a Chinese food restaurant, and keep the original name!"

CHAPTER TWELVE

Is Owning a Franchise the Best Thing for You?

There is a way you can go into business and have a support system already in place to help you: buy a franchise. There are franchises engaging in a variety of businesses, selling both goods and services. Pets, employment agencies, automobile tires, athletic shoes, eyeglasses, fitness salons—you name it, you can probably buy a franchise to open. Names of franchises that are household words: Kentucky Fried Chicken and McDonald's, Meineke Discount Muffler Shops, Century 21 Realty, and Snelling & Snelling employment agencies. The total sales of goods and services made by franchises were almost $400 billion in 1984. There were almost 450,000 separate franchise outlets.

If you have little business experience, pay special attention to the following sections. Buying a reputable franchise can be an excellent way to learn more about the business world as your franchisor teaches you how to be successful. If you are successful, you may later sell the franchise and start another business from scratch, using all that you've learned.

Buying a Franchise.

When you buy a franchise, you are really buying the rights to do business using the name and logo of an already existing company. The franchisor provides you with a business plan that has already been worked out for you.

Beyond that, what you get in assistance or advertising or guidelines varies from franchisor to franchisor. Usually certain restrictions and costs are part of the agreement. For instance, a franchise will restrict the changes you can make in its already proven selling format. If you want to open and operate a Century 21 franchise, you and your realtors will all have to wear the gold blazers that are identified with that chain. If you open a McDonald's, you must put up golden arches and serve what the company tells you to serve.

You usually pay an initial fee for the right to be a franchise, and monthly fees thereafter, which widely vary from one franchise to another. You are willing to pay these annual and monthly fees because in exchange the company gives you a lot of information and makes you smart about how they have made other franchises successful. This information and framework enhances your own chance of success.

There Can Be a Lot of Advantages to Owning a Franchise.

With a franchise, you as an individual voluntarily enter into an arrangement with a large organization. The knowledge and skill of that corporation, combined with your own ambition and autonomy, can give you the best of both worlds. Ideally, the franchisor is like a wise, benevolent partner who helps conduct your business. It wants you to prosper so you can continue to pay the ongoing royalties and fees that enrich the franchisor's coffers: if all goes well, you *both* benefit.

When a large organization and you, the entrepreneur, work together, advertising costs are often borne by all the other franchises so that you can build a national name without having to spend a fortune of your own money. Also, banded together you have the benefits of the economics of scale: you are able to supply your stationery, your office furniture, and your inventory at the lower cost big buying clout can give you.

Often the greatest advantage of a well-known franchise chain is the name you get to use. It was the advertising clout of Century 21 that prompted Barbara Einbinder to buy a franchise. "The main attraction for my husband and me was a large company that could afford to advertise on TV," says Einbinder. Today she and her husband have six offices in New Jersey with 150 salespeople working for them.

When the name of your franchise is a household word, you spend less time proving yourself or explaining what you do. If you open a Wendy's restaurant, everyone already knows exactly what you sell. The same is true with Radio Shack or Roto-Rooter or H & R Block. Because you have been presold to your customers, more of them come to you automatically. Not all franchises are household words, of course; and if not, more of the responsibility for explaining your business to customers falls on your shoulders.

To sum up: With a franchise your chances of succeeding are better because you are not in the position of reinventing the wheel. Your business has already been thought through for you, so there is less you need to learn the hard way. The franchise trains you, helps you, answers your questions, and generally tells you how to run a successful business.

When a Franchise Is a Good Idea.

Buying a franchise brings you a supportive team and information. This can be crucial if you are entering a business you don't already thoroughly understand. For instance, Jeanne Kennedy, who now owns six Meineke Discount Muffler Shops, opted for a franchise because she was entering something new to her. "I knew I shouldn't become the owner of a business I didn't already know, so I needed the umbrella of a franchise. I didn't know what we were doing, how to equip the place, the kind of inventory to get." With her franchise, all those things were laid out for her.

If you already know the business, you may want a franchise to benefit from the advertising a large organization is able to afford. Kathleen Lison, now the owner of a Great Expectations franchise in Portland, Oregon, had already operated a company to match single male and female clients using videotaping before she bought the franchise. "First of all, there's a built-in stigma to this business: 'If I have to go to a dating service, there's got to be something wrong with me,' is what my clients think before they come in. I was fighting tooth and nail against that. Great Expectations is the Cadillac of the industry, and they have established credibility through all the major media," she explains.

Franchising Is No Panacea.

Before buying a franchise begins to sound too good to be true, you should know that life with a franchisor is not necessarily a bed of roses. There can be problems. Franchisors can let you down. For instance, when Beverly Garland bought a Howard Johnson franchise to build a hotel in Hollywood, California, Howard Johnson was not the giant it is today. Garland was left on her own while the franchisor scrambled to provide assistance, which was sometimes woefully inadequate. "We asked them to send us a book on how to train our maids. They sent us one page, which said that maids should come in on time and clean the rooms. Big help. But since then they've gotten a lot better. It has grown as we've grown. Now they have training programs and everything."

One of the problems you have when your franchise has a well-known name is that if the franchisor does not enforce high standards of all its other owners, you suffer. Frequently when a company is expanding rapidly, quality control slips, and the lack of high-quality goods or services in other places reflects poorly on you. After all, if the name you paid to use gets tarnished elsewhere, then *you* have to work harder to persuade your customers that your particular franchise is still good.

What looks like an opportunity to jump on the bandwagon of a hot new franchisor can turn into a nightmare of learning the hard way, should the rapidly growing company be unable to deliver the promised backup. Says one franchisee: "When I tried to get help from headquarters, there wasn't any to be found. It made me realize what a franchisor really is. They can, but they're not obliged to lay out a lot of money for a program that's good for us. The responsibility falls back on me even though the franchisor has told me they will do it."

So one of your chief vulnerabilities when you buy a franchise is that you are dependent on the company to follow through on its promises. If it lets you down, you have to swim on your own, while continuing to pay your contractually obligatory fees.

You are also at the mercy of your franchisor if it exercises poor judgment. One franchisee discovered this the hard way. "We can't get delivery on an ingredient they specify and they won't let us substitute, so we're caught in the middle. We lose money. They have hard and fast rules and are not flexible. The inspectors they hire to check out stores are all in their early twenties. They come in for an hour and make a lot of judgments, usually wrong."

There is nothing magic about franchising. No matter how hard both you and your franchisor work together, you may still have to struggle to survive. Honey Levine, who now has a successful Century 21 operation, recalls, "It took a long time to break even. I remember—I don't ever want to forget—once the paperboy came to my office to collect $3 for the week's papers, and I went to the back of the office and cried because I didn't have it. Real estate is not a cash flow business—I didn't even know what the term *meant* in those days." Levine laughs grimly. "It took close to six or eight months to start seeing money come in."

Investigate Your Franchise Before You Buy.

Franchising is a general word that covers an enormous range of businesses and almost as many different kinds of agreements between you and the franchisor. Some are for ten or twenty years, and some are for as long as you want them. Some franchisors exact a percentage of sales from their franchisees, while others require a flat fee regardless of sales. Some advertise heavily, while others leave it up to you.

There are well over a thousand franchisors. You should investigate a variety of them before you settle on one. And you should do the necessary homework to protect yourself against the unscrupulous or less reliable ones. Never forget that if the parent company goes out of business, you are out of business, too.

The first step you should take is to contact the International Franchise Association:

> International Franchise Association
> 1025 Connecticut Avenue, N.W.
> Washington, D.C. 20036

The IFA is a trade association of reputable franchise companies. It routinely provides lists of its member companies with addresses and estimated start-up costs. The IFA will also provide you with literature aimed at making you a knowledgeable shopper among franchisors.

You are fortunate if the state in which you are thinking about buying a franchise has passed a franchise law. Under such a law franchisors are required to tell any prospective franchisee about any illegal shenanigans in their past, particularly fraud. To find out where your state office is or to discover other information about a franchisor, contact:

Federal Trade Commission
Sixth and Pennsylvania Avenue, N.W.
Washington, D.C. 20580
Telephone: (202) 523-1753

The following states have passed a franchise law: California, Hawaii, Illinois, Indiana, Maryland, Michigan, Minnesota, New York, North Dakota, Oregon, Rhode Island, South Dakota, Virginia, Washington, and Wisconsin. Additional states are considering a legislation. Check with the FTC to see if your state has recently passed a franchise law.

Between the Federal Trade Commission and the International Franchise Association you can arm yourself with a wealth of information about any franchisors you are interested in. Do not bypass these crucial resources.

Remember, almost anything that can go wrong will go wrong, which is why it is so important you spend the time to research a franchise before you buy one and spend the money for good accounting and legal advice.

Where to Begin.

Once a particular franchise arouses your interest, you must begin to evaluate it carefully. First of all, look at the industry the franchise is in. Paying no heed to the franchisor's words, what does your *common sense* tell you? Is the industry a growing one, or do you think it has peaked? For instance, with the proliferation of food chains, do you think you can meet the rosy financial projections a food franchisor promises you? If it is a new food chain, do you feel it can compete with the already established chains whose revenues give them formidable advertising clout?

You want to get yourself in an industry that is positioned for stable growth, like the fast-food market, which gains popularity as more women like you open their own businesses and have less time to cook. If you can find a franchise in an industry that's growing, it's easier for you as a franchise owner to prosper. When your industry is booming, it is easier for you to boom right along with it.

Ideally you should pick a franchise that suits your temperament. If you love animals, look at pet shop franchises before you consider an employment agency, but be especially careful here, as many have damaged reputations. If you love mechanics, look at automotive supply and maintenance companies before you look at a dating service. If you love flowers, look at a floral franchise before you consider a tax preparation service.

Don't be quick to settle. Your commitment to a franchise will be for several years at least. You should not decide to buy one in haste.

The easiest way to check out a franchisor is to talk to some of its other franchisees. "The most important thing when you're looking to buy a franchise is not what's in the contract," says franchise expert Jack McBirney, who heads the Franchise Consulting Group in Boston. "The contract is important, of course, but it might be interpreted differently from what you think. So you must talk to existing franchise owners. Ask them if the franchisor has done what they said they were going to do, if their financial results are what they hoped for, if they get support from the franchisor, and what the problems are."

You'll find out more about a company's strengths and weaknesses from its franchisees in a few hours than you will from spending weeks poring over paperwork. The expense of making a few telephone calls to current franchisees in nearby towns will be well worth the money.

Check Out the Product.

Visit some existing franchisees and see what you think of the operation. See if you think the concept as "cloned" by the franchisor is effective. Estimate the costs of the products and evaluate whether you think the products will continue to be price-competitive.

Find out who makes the product. Is the source of production reliable? If they go out of business, can another one be found quickly to continue supply without disrupting service?

Also consider whether the product or service is trendy. Even though it sold well in California, will it play in Des Moines, where you are considering opening the franchise?

Scrutinize the Company.

Do your homework before you spend any time with a company you are considering. Be sure you do not sign anything committing yourself before you have checked out the company completely. A company that is anxious to sign you up without checking your credentials and scrutinizing your own background carefully is questionable. Any franchisor that rushes you is highly suspect. Any that seems too eager to get the initial fee should also be considered suspect.

When you contact a franchisor you will receive a kit providing the standard sales pitch and many promises. Do not take it at face value. First of all, since you are going to need an attorney to complete the negotiations anyway, ask him to run a credit check on the company and find out if it is privately held, public, or a subsidiary of a public company.

If the company is publicly held, it is very simple for you to get information about it from your local library, which subscribes to *Value Line* and *Standard & Poor's*, two respected financial services that follow major companies. If the company is a subsidiary of a larger corporation, study the parent organization as well as the specific subsidiary you are interested in. Is the parent company committed to the business, or does it have a history of writing off ill-fated ventures?

If the company is privately held, it is not obligated to outsiders to disclose its true intentions and financial strength. If it is private, you must intensively research it on your own, canvassing its existing franchisees as well as the competition. If the company claims a certain number of outlets, ask for a list of the owners. Randomly check with a few to validate the company's claims. Further, verify the length of time the company claims to have been in business. Ask for the business backgrounds of its officers and directors. Check with the Better Business Bureau in towns where it does a great deal of business to see if complaints have been filed.

Don't take anything for granted. Be as jaded as the bankers who insist on driving out to the factory to be sure it actually exists. It's *your* money you are investing, and no one is going to have your interests in mind as much as you do. Whatever you do, do not act in haste. A franchise is a ten- to twenty-year commitment.

Probe the Profits.

Don't accept the profit projections the franchisor provides you as necessarily honest or true. Ask your accountant to prepare independent projections and compare them.

If your franchisor provides you with financial projections, ask where they came from. Are they imaginary, or do they have a basis in fact, compiled from the current experience of other franchisees? Be critical of the time periods included in projections, always remembering that the franchisor wants you to view the potential profitability of a franchise in the best possible light. Don't automatically accept the past two or five years' performance of some franchisees as a prediction of how your franchise will fare for the next two or five years. Investigate to see whether the bloom is off the rose.

Check with other franchisees and see if they believe the projections you have been given are realistic. Compare yours with profit potentials estimated for them; also ask whether the franchisor prepared a realistic forecast for them. Compare your projections against the actual performance of other franchisees.

When you are analyzing the profits, don't forget to take into account your own salary if you are going to be working in the business. Make sure the profits and the salary are adequate to reimburse you for the extra risk and investment you incur when you open the franchise. Would you do better by investing the money in your own independent service business out of your home? *You should consider this carefully.*

Examine the Cost.

Compare the cost of a franchise with what it would take to begin a separate business of your own, including promotion, advertising, and operation.

Never forget that the franchisor has no intention of giving away anything. Its only interest is in continuing to grow itself. If you serve its interests, all well and good. But it has not the slightest intention of losing money on you. Be specific about any services it promises you in the future—are they included, or are there charges? What are the charges?

After the initial franchise fee, the franchisor may want payment and reimbursement for marketing and advertising in one of two ways, either as a flat fee, which you pay on a monthly basis, or as a percentage of your profits. The later usually ranges from 4 to 10 percent of sales. But do not assume the fees and royalties are written in stone. Negotiate to see if there is any flexibility.

The cost of constructing a new operation itself varies. A Häagen-Dazs ice cream installation costs about $125,000 to construct and stock with inventory, on top of a $25,000 fee. A Wendy's outlet, including the purchase of the land and the $20,000 fee, could cost around $750,000. Because the costs are so high, the two firms request that certain minimum cash assets be available from prospective franchisees. Häagen-Dazs requires that $100,000 be on hand in cash, stocks and bonds, or some other liquid asset. Wendy's suggests a personal net worth of at least $250,000, with $150,000 in liquid assets available for the business.

But business franchises are not necessarily prohibitively expensive. Travel Agents International says that after you supply your own premises and overhead, it will supply an office package for you for $12,500; it charges a franchise fee of $20,000.

Costs vary from business to business. With such a wide range, it is worth your time to do extensive homework.

It is important that you check out what is specifically requested in contracts. Nail down precisely what is meant when "fees" are mentioned. Examine any clauses stating the circumstances under which the fee structure can be increased. Determine whether or not you are going to be charged for bookkeeping and marketing services on a continuing basis. Find out if there are minimum inventory requirements regardless of sales. Don't forget to investigate other charges the franchisor may assume you will personally bear the burden of, such as fees for zoning permits and local licenses to do business.

Your costs are the most important considerations when evaluating a deal. It is best to call in a bright, aggressive accountant to assist you. Don't skimp on accounting fees when you investigate a franchise, particularly if you are inexperienced in business matters. A franchise is a contract that will entail your investing sizable funds. Good professional assistance will be the best investment you can make.

Peruse the Provisions.

There are provisions in any franchise contract. Read them carefully. Some may refer to your own involvement in the business. For instance, to qualify for a Wendy's franchise, you "must live within a fifty-mile radius of the restaurant and devote 100 percent of your business time and effort to the development and operation" of your Wendy's franchise. On the other hand, some franchisors do not care whether you live on the same side of the country where your franchise is located.

There are also provisions about the appearance of your operation. Your franchisor can be as finicky as the contract allows. It can monitor the quality and quantity of your goods, the kinds of advertising and promotion you undertake, and how the outlet is designed and built originally.

"Restrictions may not be onerous, but you should be aware of them," counsels franchise expert Jack McBirney. "They affect things like what products you can carry and what you cannot. For instance, at Have A Heart (a franchise that sells heart-shaped items and objects with hearts on them) you can't sell car batteries."

Provisions may be restrictive, but generally their intention is to protect all the franchisees. Frequently they deal with quality control, so that one outlet cannot taint the reputation of all others bearing the same name. For instance, if you noticed one fast-food operation was dirty, you might balk at going to any of their other outlets.

Elaine Powers manufactures exercise equipment that the franchisees can buy, although they aren't required to. However, Elaine Powers must approve of any equipment you go out and purchase someplace else. "They can't just go out and buy pogo sticks," says Elizabeth Browning, who works for the Elaine Powers organization in addition to owning two franchises.

Just as good professional accounting advice is worth every penny when you are analyzing the costs of a franchise, good legal advice is essential when you evaluate the restrictions in a franchise contract.

Don't fall in love with the idea before you know all the rules. You should enter the contract with your *head*, not your heart. You should also do some honest soul-searching about how you are going to react with your franchisor constantly looking over your shoulder.

Terms and Transfer.

A franchise contract is for a specified amount of time, usually ten to twenty years. Generally longer is better.

Make sure of your options to renew. You want these options to be favorable to you. After all, if you are going to work to build a profitable undertaking, you may want to continue it for a lifetime.

You should also examine exactly how binding the renewal contract is. If the franchisor is purchased by another company, will the new owner be required to honor your renewal options? Make sure the agreement is ironclad, so that regardless of who is in charge of the franchisor, your options are protected.

Find out in advance whether the franchisor is required to buy back the facility (if you built it) and the inventory and other related assets, in case you or it decides not to continue in the business. Further, check to see whether you have a right to transfer the ownership of the franchise to your family in case of your death or retirement.

It is important to investigate your right to sell. In the event of your death, you want your estate to be able to sell it. *How you get out of the contract is as important as how you get in.* Have both your accountant and your attorney verify that there is an exit permitting you to sell without being the loser in the deal.

Financing Your Franchise.

Getting a banker to listen to your request for money is easier when you have a major franchisor behind you. The success rates of Howard Johnson, Century 21, or McDonald's franchisees may make it considerably easier to get a loan. Bankers understand the extent of help that major, widely known franchisors give their outlets.

Your franchisor can give you assistance in other ways. "One thing that helped us a lot was that Howard Johnson decided to lease and run the restaurant from us," reports Beverly Garland, who owns a Hollywood, California, Howard Johnson hotel. "That was great because our bankers knew then that we'd have a certain amount of rent from Howard Johnson each month."

You may hope to recoup your initial investment in three or four years, but if you have problems, it may take as many as five. Such was the instance of Beverly Garland. "It was a terrible struggle. We did it on a shoestring, and by the time we opened we had one guest. Believe me, I've folded sheets in my day."

Well-Known Franchise Chains

Arthur Murray International Inc.—Coral Gables, FL (dance instructors)

Athlete's Foot Marketing Association, Inc.—Pittsburgh, PA (active wear)

Budget Rent A Car Corporation—Chicago, IL (car rental)

Carvel Corporation—Yonkers, NY (ice cream stores)

Century 21—Irvine, CA (real estate brokers)

Computerland Corporation—Hayward, CA (retail computer stores)

Conroy's Florists—Culver City, CA (full-service florists and mass merchandiser)

Dunkin' Donuts, Inc.—Randolph, MA (doughnuts, bakery products, and beverages)

Elaine Powers Figure Salons, Inc.—Milwaukee, WI (women's figure control)

Flowerama of America, Inc.—Waterloo, IA (retail floral and gift shops)

Goodyear Tire & Rubber Company—Akron, OH (selling tires)

Häagen-Dazs Shoppe Company, Inc.—Englewood Cliffs, NJ (ice cream shops)

H & R Block, Inc.—Kansas City, MO (income tax preparers)

Howard Johnson Company—North Quincy, MA (hotels and restaurants)

Lawn Doctor, Inc.—Matawan, NJ (automated lawn services)

McDonald's Corporation—Oak Brook, IL (fast-food restaurants)

Meineke Discount Muffler Shops—Houston, TX (muffler shop)

Petland, Inc.—Chillocothe, OH (pet stores)

Pier 1 Imports, Inc.—Ft. Worth, TX (home furnishings, gifts)

Radio Shack—Ft. Worth, TX (consumer electronics stores)

Roto-Rooter Corporation—Des Moines, IA (sewer, drain, and pipe cleaning)

Searle Optical—Dallas, TX (retailers of eyewear)

Snelling & Snelling, Inc.—Sarasota, FL (employment agencies)

Travel Agents International—Seminole, FL (travel agencies)

Wendy's International, Inc.—Dublin, OH (fast-food restaurants)

Off-Beat Franchise Chains

Balloon Bouquets—Belmont, MA (inflated balloons with a variety of attached streamers and gifts)

Blackmon, Mooring Steamatic, Inc.—Grand Prairie, TX (disaster specialist—fire work and water removal; residence and commercial carpet cleaning)

Delphi Stained Glass Centers—Lansing, MI (stained-glass supplies and glasses)

Getting to Know You International Ltd.—Westbury, NY (new homeowner welcome service)

Great Expectations—Los Angeles, CA (video dating services)

Gymboree Corporation—Burlingame, CA (parent participation program to develop early motor and learning skills in kids three months to four years)

Have A Heart—Boston, MA (retail shop selling heart theme items)

Left Hand World—San Francisco, CA (left-handed items for lefties)

Sara Care Franchise Corporation—El Paso, TX (sitting services—companion, baby, house, and hospital)

Tender Sender—Vancouver, WA (gift wrapping, packaging, and shipment services)

United Dignity—Nashville, TN (funeral homes)

Examples of Start-Up Costs of Franchises

Delphi Stained Glass Centers

Franchise fee	$ 7,000
Security deposit for lease	3,000
Inventory	30,000
Leasehold improvements; carpet, fixtures	10,000
Minimum working capital	10,000
	$60,000

Ground Round Restaurants
(owned by Howard Johnson Company)

	FROM	TO
License fee...	$ 30,000	$ 30,000
Land..	200,000	350,000
Building	350,000	500,000
Equipment	225,000	265,000
Liquor license (varies from state to state)		
Sign...	14,000	14,000
Working capital....................................	25,000	25,000
Fees, licenses, permits........................	50,000	50,000
	$894,000	$1,234,000

Häagen-Dazs Shoppe Company, Inc.

Franchise fee	$ 25,500	$ 25,500
Construction costs	45,000	85,000
Refrigeration and other equipment	20,000	25,000
Initial inventory..................................	8,500	10,000
	$ 99,000	$ 145,500

McDonald's Corporation

Franchise fee	$ 12,500	$ 12,500
Security deposit (refundable when expires)	15,000	15,000
Kitchen equipment..............................	135,000	135,000
Seating and decor...............................	35,000	35,000
Taxes, delivery, and installation...........	18,000	26,000
Cash register system	10,000	31,000
Miscellaneous equipment, construction, landscaping, operating cash, safe, first month's rent, training, preopening expenses	50,000	75,000
	$275,500	$ 329,500

Meineke Discount Muffler Shops, Inc.

License fee, equipment, inventory, marketing, and site selection		$ 66,000

	FROM	TO
Travel Agents International		
Franchise fee	$ 20,000	
Furniture, signs, carpet, and so forth...	12,500	
	$ 32,500	
United Dignity		
Franchise fee	$ 15,000	$ 15,000
Leasing/owning facilities, equipment, and vehicles	75,000	170,000
Recommended working capital............	25,000	25,000
	$115,000	$ 210,000
Wendy's International, Inc.		
Technical Assistance fee......................	$ 20,000	$ 20,000
Land.....................................	100,000	300,000
Building	175,000	225,000
Site improvement...............................	50,000	150,000
Equipment	135,000	160,000
Miscellaneous (initial inventory, working capital, taxes, insurance, utility deposit, licenses)	32,000	49,000
	$512,000	$ 904,000

Strategies for Coping

CHAPTER THIRTEEN

Being Entrepreneurial Has Its Own Stresses: How to Cope

Discovering you don't want to work for anyone but yourself can be very stressful. But running your own business is no picnic, either—it has its own set of worries. You are out in the world and you are completely responsible for yourself. There's no regular paycheck, no guaranteed health benefits, no office space provided, and no one else to blame if you fail.

This can be downright scary and nerve-racking at times. You may toss and turn for weeks before making a decision that is critical to your success. You may work harder than you ever dreamed getting your business off the ground.

It's important to anticipate the stresses you will experience and prepare yourself for them. It's also critical that you not isolate yourself, but share your problems and discuss your opportunities with others who are also running their own companies. Moreover, you should examine yourself to see what kinds of personal habits you can develop to help you alleviate the stresses of being out on your own.

Ultimately, even though being entrepreneurial entails risks and stress, you'll probably find the challenges exhilarating and the rewards downright fun.

Sleepless Nights Come with the Territory.

It is only normal to be scared when you start your own business. You are haunted by the possibility that your business will come apart at the seams and fail. "I used to worry what would happen if no one came to my seminars," notes eminently successful investment firm chief Venita vanCaspel.

You may find yourself worrying about every aspect of your undertaking, particularly when you are involved in a large project with the possibility of great success and failure.

"Sometimes I stay up all night," admits Harriet Winter, the New York designer.

"Sleepless nights come with the territory," declares New York psychologist Dr. Ella Lasky. "There are real stresses when you're an entrepreneur. Appropriate stress creates an appropriate reaction." The appropriate reaction is to work harder. In fact, paranoia and pessimism about your company's prospects *may* be the very stimuli that propel you to success. The more scared you are, the harder you may work to succeed.

Distress Signals.

However, you should keep in mind that there are a number of red flags that should trigger you to take action to regain a positive attitude if you are becoming too fatalistic. For instance, if you are isolating yourself from other people for long periods of time, take heed. Isolating yourself may allow you to dwell on perceived business difficulties. Spending time with supportive friends can broaden your perspective and improve your state of mind.

Overreacting to stresses consistently or gaining/losing weight rapidly is an indication you are not coping effectively with the difficulties facing you. Moreover, if you feel under the weather all the time and not yourself, you may need to improve your outlook on your business. If you are tired every morning or have a vague malaise you can't whip, take a vacation until you feel restored. Then reexamine your business to find the reason for your mental or physical fatigue.

If you are depressed a great deal, you're probably feeling overwhelmed by your undertaking. Try to analyze the source of your depression and take steps to change it. If it's because business is bad, you must try to take a more constructive approach or find a new business. It's important that you not consider a failure in your business to be a failure of yourself. *Remember that errors in judgment are not flaws in your character.*

If you find you cannot shake your depression and distress yourself, seek professional help before you completely lose your perspective on your business.

Tonics and Touchstones.

Regardless of what business you enter, it is unrealistic to expect things to run smoothly all the time. They don't. The nature of doing business is that, regardless of who you are and what you do, you are going to encounter tough times. Market changes, employee errors, interest-rate hikes, overprojections of market share, undercapitalization and cash binds, and rapid growth—there are so many things that can burden the woman in charge.

The best way to deal with the many stresses you'll have when you run your own company is to be honest about the pressure you're experiencing and to approach it in a way that will enable you to operate at maximum effectiveness. Don't deny your stress, and don't pretend it doesn't exist.

Train yourself to deal with intense pressure before you ever encounter it. Then, should you ever face a really dire situation, you will be able to react effectively.

Name your demon. One way to prepare for disaster in advance is to develop a Worst Possible Case scenario—what would happen if everything that could go wrong did go wrong. Then form a contingency plan about how you would act if those things should occur. Suggests psychotherapist Dr. Edith Byer, "Analyze yourself. Say to yourself, 'Okay, what's the worst thing that can happen? What will I feel like if it happens?' Name the worst things. What would these situations feel like to you? As you look at them, figure out what your options would be. Think, 'When I lose X then I'll do Y. That would tide me through the worst part. . . .' "

Naming your demons will probably give you a sense of relief. If you've already faced and mastered them in your imagination, it reduces the terror they hold for you.

Old glories. Another way to reduce stress and increase your confidence is to reflect on your previous achievements. Don't dismiss them as inconsequential. It is healthy to recall your past successes and the exact steps you took which created that success for you. Much of success shares a common root. Often it lies in your overall attitude, up-against-the-wall resourcefulness, and the timing of your response. When things are tough, don't hesitate to remind yourself, "If I handled that fiasco last year, I'm sure I can deal with this one today."

If you had a retail store and your inventory didn't move a few years ago and you came up with a spectacular advertising campaign that totally reversed the situation and sold the store out, review your notes and see exactly what steps you took to achieve that success. If you managed to drum up five important new clients three years ago with a series of well-orchestrated cocktail parties, review exactly how you compiled your guest lists and who your biggest boosters were.

Leave other options open. If you're even slightly faint of heart, don't pour all your resources into one big commitment. If you do, the possibility exists that you could be pushed into the proverbial corner. Instead, venture slowly into business, always keeping reserves on the side—just in case.

The riskier the business, the more important it is that you venture into it gingerly, exploring its pace and rhythm while keeping a few other pots simmering on back burners. The peace of mind you gain can be marvelous when you know that if one venture fails totally, you immediately have other viable options available.

Put the blame in the right place. If everything does go wrong and you woefully misjudge your marketplace, what are you going to do? Sit in the corner and punish yourself? Hide?

Nonsense! If you feel you've made a serious error in judgment, look at the background of your error and analyze where you went wrong. Was it indeed an error in judgment, or was it simply one of those things only a clairvoyant could have foreseen? Don't chastise yourself for making human errors. Time spent punishing yourself is wasted.

"Women tend to blame themselves too much," notes psychotherapist Dr. Ella Lasky. "They really shouldn't be too hard on themselves. They shouldn't blame themselves for things they couldn't control."

Lists. Probably the most utilized organizer lies in your practicing the art of list making. Once the list of things to remember has been made, you, the harried entrepreneur, can put your mind at ease, focusing on the work at hand, reassured that you're not going to forget anything.

Keep a pencil and pad on hand at all times—even at your bedside. Keeping tabs on all the small details of running the business can free your mind to deal more effectively with its larger issues.

Even a plethora of lists can be effective. "Lists are the essence of my business," notes a caterer. "The thing that sets me apart is my attention to detail. Lists take care of all the details. If I didn't have them, I'd never get a decent night's sleep."

Symbolism. Lists can also be used symbolically. When you get depressed or upset, write down everything that is troubling you—*everything*. Then divide the list into two parts: make one a list of things you can do something about and the other of things you can't. Then take the list you can't do anything about and slowly set fire to it and watch it burn. Then get to work on the doable.

Symbolic acts can go far beyond ridding yourself of the worry over things you can't control. When you play tennis, smack the ball with all you've got and mentally imagine you are hitting your competitor.

Keep Your Worries in Perspective.

Before you say anything to anyone about your worries, it might be best to sit down and have a conversation with yourself. Sometimes looking in a mirror helps.

"I have a lot of mirror talks," admits one very successful entrepreneur. "I tell myself I'm an idiot to be so uptight. I tell myself if something is doable, then I can do it. I don't usually really believe myself, but maybe it helps."

Another entrepreneur who gets angry when mistakes occur privately lectures herself. "Calm down, calm down," she instructs while also measuring her breathing carefully. Only after she has lowered her pulse in private does she confront the person responsible for her troubles.

Sometimes it is useful if the talk you have with yourself is pre-rehearsed. A highly skilled consultant reports that she still has difficulty charging as much as she should for her services. She has memorized several admonitions which she routinely whispers to herself at the suggestion of a colleague. "How could you be ashamed about asking for the money you've earned?" is one she repeats to herself when she balks at charging steep fees. The exercise has been useful: higher retainers she has collected have completely compensated for some cash flow problems she used to encounter.

Rena Tarbet, a supersaleswoman for Mary Kay Cosmetics, has a standard speech she gives herself: "I remind myself delays are not deathly. Pressures are not permanent. Failures are not fatal. Life is what you make it. I don't believe in PLOM—Poor Little Old Me."

Get active. One of the healthiest reactions to stress is leaving the office and indulging in physical exercise. Physical activity pushes your problems to your subconscious while you concentrate on a sport. *Any sport is better than none.*

Physical exercise not only provides you with a change of pace from your work life, it also revitalizes a body that can get bogged down from sitting in an office chair for twelve hours a day. Moreover, keeping fit helps you look more successful. If you are energetic and look healthy, people tend to believe you can do what you say you will do.

Self-pampering. Pampering your body can revitalize your mind. Hot baths can relax you. A session with a masseuse can stretch out your back. A facial can be stimulating. A day at a beauty clinic can make you look better—and feel rejuvenated and positive again.

One woman who suffered a serious business setback says, "I treated myself with kindness. I had done my best and it didn't work. Before I wanted to start over I wanted to be good to me." Every day for a week she took off in the morning for a facial and a massage. Only then did she plunge back into her business full steam ahead.

Be religious. If you are religious, don't be shy about it. Some of the most successful women in the country are frank and open about their deep belief in God. Religion is a perennial solace, especially during times of stress.

Find People You Can Lean On.

One of the strongest needs of the entrepreneur is a network of friends and advisors to talk to. Without other people's input it's very difficult to know how well you're doing or what you could do that you're not. You cannot know everything all by yourself, and you need people to talk to. It is essential that those people you rely on be basically supportive, because as an entrepreneur you tend to be your worst critic. You don't need to have someone second-guessing you. What you need are people who, although not Pollyannas, will be constructive and resourceful in helping you meet your business challenges.

Lean on your friends. Let them withdraw the sting from failure and the pain from disaster. If you are married, your husband can be an invaluable sounding board and source of support. But most important, seek out other people in similar businesses and talk shop with them. Finding out how someone coped in a similar situation can be invaluable. Listening to how others made mistakes can help you avoid them.

Systematically build a network of people to talk to about your business. Expand it to include a variety of viewpoints. Don't exclude men from your support team. *You need all the input you can get.*

CHAPTER FOURTEEN

You Can Avoid the Stress of Taking Giant Steps

There is no reason why the move into entrepreneurship has to be traumatic and sudden. It is not necessary to rush head-on into the unknowns of owning and running your own business. Ideally, you can ease yourself into your own business slowly, preparing so well in advance that the transition is comfortable. Moreover, the better planned your venture and the better you are prepared to run it, the more likely your chances of success.

There are a variety of things you can do. You can learn about a business by working for someone else before you attempt it on your own. You can start a venture on the side while continuing to draw a salary from a job you hold, so that you have an opportunity to test the viability of a concept before you burn any bridges behind you.

Use Your Job as Training to Go into Your Own Business.

As stated before, you should never go into a business unless you have already learned a great deal about the operation you are getting into. One of the easiest ways to learn is to go to work in a company that does what you want to do and learn to do it at their expense before you attempt it on your own.

Even if it is your intention to be entrepreneurial, a job working for someone else may help lay the groundwork for your success. The contacts you make in your employment can provide a client list for your future business, as was the case with Debbie Storrs, now president of that successful collection agency. Storrs worked for the police, several banks, and as a security supervisor for a retail store chain before she founded her collection service in Houston. "I knew that in your twenties you work for other people and pay your dues. You get a skill, background, and experience credits. In your thirties you become an entrepreneur," she says. "It's very logical."

You must exercise patience while you are learning a business. Mary Kay Ash of Mary Kay Cosmetics did. Says Ash, "I had twenty-five years of watching companies do things I thought were wrong." Expert in the ins and outs of direct sales, she was able to found a company that avoided many of the pitfalls of competitors.

You might even become a deliberate job hopper while honing your skills, spending time at one corporation until you learn the job you want to know about and then moving to another one, gathering skill after skill and comparing styles of management in similar operations.

You Can Go into Competition with Your Previous Employer.

You might go to work for a firm with the explicit intention of someday going into competition with it. You shouldn't announce your intentions, of course. You don't say, "I'm here to learn everything you know and then give you a run for your money."

What you do is learn everything you can. Learn from your employer's mistakes. Learn how to avoid them.

Usually when you move out and become directly competitive with your employer, there are bad feelings. Your ex-boss feels you have betrayed him or her. You may even be regarded as a thief who has stolen ideas and contacts. Says Susan Bang, who after she started her own public relations undertaking vied against her old employer for an account and won: "They're definitely not happy for me. They didn't want to see me be a success."

Learn What You Can Take with You Before You Leave a Company.

When you leave a company to start your own, there may be restrictions as to what you can take with you. You should never sign a noncompete contract wherein you promise not to work for a competitor or go into direct competition yourself with your employer. "It is to your advantage not to sign anything that restricts you in using information you learn while you are at a company," advises Washington, D.C., attorney Linda Smith.

If you are asked to sign a standard covenant not to compete, check first with an independent attorney. "The broader the covenant, the harder it is to enforce," notes Smith. Study your employment contract and get legal advice in advance of any actions you take.

Before you leave, try to ascertain precisely what they consider to be "proprietary." If the firm is large enough to have its own personnel department you can visit the office and ask what the company considers to be exclusively its own.

Check around with industry and trade associations in your area of interest and assess the standard industry practices. What is proprietary varies with the circumstances. For instance, if you work for a personnel agency and decide to start your own, they would no doubt consider their client list to be proprietary information. But if you were to take a list of people you interviewed while hiring for the personnel department of a company in another business, that list might not be proprietary.

It is best to approach the transition from employee to competitor in a clean-cut manner similar to that taken by Lynn Morgenroth, who left a public relations agency to begin her own. "I didn't contact clients before I left. I gave notice and said, 'Whatever happens, I'm going to be a competitor, so I better leave today.' The next day I called the clients and explained the situation and made a pitch. But I never said a bad word about Bob (her previous boss), nor did he about me."

Some Jobs Are Better Training Grounds than Others.

Not every job is a training ground. If you are doing clerical work for a giant company, it's not very likely you will gain any contacts that would be helpful to you in starting a small restaurant. What you should do instead is find a job working for a restaurant and learn the business from the inside. At the same time, you are meeting customers who someday might be yours.

By the same token, if you are interested in public relations, go to work for a firm already successful in the business and become a star account executive. The contacts you make with the clients will be the basis for your being recommended highly when you branch out on your own.

Further, smaller companies offer better training opportunities than larger ones. The ideal company in which to learn a business is one where everyone's duties change whenever the pressure is on. You are exposed to every aspect of the business, and this across-the-boards exposure can be invaluable helping you face the realities of running your own business.

Positions and Industries That Offer You a Broad View of Business and Business a Good View of You

Position	Industry	Advantage
CPA/auditor	Accounting firm	You make contacts at all the companies you audit.
Salesperson	Radio or TV local stations	You call on the heads of local businesses.
Salesperson	Aircraft	You call on heads of larger local and national businesses.
Account executive	Public relations firm	You get attention from the heads of major companies.
Staff	Congress or Senate	Perceived power by all the folks back home. National connections.
Staff	Mayoralty or state government	You brush shoulders with local business heads.
Staff	Trade organizations	High recognition among industry members.
Account executive	Advertising	Contact with decision-makers at client companies.
Salesperson	Large computers	Contact with decision-makers in charge of large budgets.
Salesperson	Commercial real estate	Contact with company owners.
Manager	Prominent restaurant	Contact with locally prominent business people.
Manager	Country club	Contact with locally prominent citizens.

Reporter	Local newspaper	Broad recognition throughout the community.
Supervisor/ trainer	Any business	The people you train know how good you are.
Buyer	Department store	Contact with key suppliers.
Buyer	Nonretail business	Your suppliers know what a tough deal you negotiate.
Repair person	Electronics company	Your customers know how good you are.
Teacher	Adult education	Your adult students perceive you as an authority.
Personnel	Any business	Access to client list for opening your own personnel agency.
Salesperson	Prominent boutique	Customers know how savvy you are.
Teacher	Local school	Parents of the children you teach know how effective you are.
Fund-raiser	Local charity	Contact with heads of all local business.
Volunteer	Political campaign	Broad contact with political people and business backers.
Sales	Cosmetics	Women you advise correctly respect you and trust you.
Sales	Real estate	People you sell for and who buy from you know how good you are.

Start Your Company on the Side.

One of the safest ways to begin a new venture is part-time, while you keep your full-time job. It gives you an opportunity to build up a clientele and test yourself in the marketplace before you cut the umbilical cord a job provides. You can work out of your home on weekends and at nights until you think the time is ripe to go it alone.

You can even incorporate a year or two before you quit. If you lay your groundwork properly, you are then able to step into an already active business.

You can move as did Flora Mattis, now a New York management consultant. She consulted on weekends and vacations while still keeping her job with ABC. Finally, having proven herself to herself, she quit and set up her own shop. She had done such an excellent job at laying the foundations for her new business that in the first year she made substantially more money than she had the previous year at her corporate job. Mattis was off and running.

Keep Your Job and Go to School.

If you want to make a dramatic change from your current employment, the best way to become appropriately qualified may be to go to school at night to learn completely new skills.

You don't have to advertise the fact that you are preparing for a change. If your boss knows you are planning to bail out, he or she may fire you before you are ready to quit or ignore you when raises are being determined.

Being a Hybrid Entrepreneur Is Less Risky.

You can avoid the trauma of being completely on your own when you go into business for yourself. There is a universe that lies halfway between being an employee and being a pure entrepreneur. This occurs, for example, in sales-related ventures where you represent a firm either part-time or full-time. You work on your own, but under the firm's auspices as its representative. You are essentially an independent contractor—a hybrid entrepreneur.

As a hybrid entrepreneur you can still take control of your life. You are able to have a flexibility and independence unknown in the nine-to-five world. Moreover, you are not hampered by traditional business assessments of your capabilities—your credentials, schooling, and experience. If you work and you are good at what you do, you are reimbursed accordingly, regardless of your style or background.

You, as a hybrid entrepreneur, could be the member of our society who comes closest to "having it all." You are responsible only for your own sales, your own sales force if you choose to build one, and your customers. The company you sell for is an entity that worries about you, about providing your supplies and rewarding you. It—not you—also has responsibilities for cash flow, financing, employees, and growth and diversification. You can concentrate simply on getting the orders.

The majority of the hybrid entrepreneurs in this country are in direct sales—you sell company-furnished products door to door or through a party system. There are approximately five million independent direct-sales people around the country, plus several more million real estate salespeople. The largest direct-selling firms are household words: Avon and Tupperware. Others are Time-Life Books, World Book, Stanhome (formerly Stanley Home Products), and Kirby vacuum cleaners.

Being a hybrid entrepreneur gives you an opportunity to structure your own hours and to make more money than you might otherwise earn. Bev Lewis, a representative for Shaklee, a company that sells foods and nutritional supplements, says, "I worked about fifteen hours a week for the first three years. I was having to take care of a baby then, so I worked around that. Now I put in over forty hours per week, but it's hard to really tell because I work a few hours here and there with constant interruptions from my daughter, who's three years old now. I have another baby due in January, but that shouldn't have any effect on my income because I can restructure the hours." Lewis expects to earn $100,000 this year.

Lewis is not an isolated success story. At Mary Kay Cosmetics, for instance, over 350 salespeople were responsible for teams that generated sales of over $1 million, earning six-figure commissions for their own accounts. Direct-sales firms usually offer additional prize incentives. Rena Tarbet, for instance, has earned eleven Cadillacs, eight fur coats, four $5,000 shopping sprees at Neiman-Marcus, and trips to "numerous resorts" in Spain, Hawaii, and the *Love Boat* in Acapulco. Tarbet has also received "lots of diamond jewelry." This is all in addition to her six-figure income.

CHAPTER FIFTEEN

How to Prepare Against Bankruptcy

Just because you read lots of success stories in this book, you can't, unfortunately, assume that nobody fails. Sadly, it happens every day. All you have to do is look around you and pay attention to all the little businesses you see folding. If you have not begun your own business yet, do your homework before you leap. No matter how much you know in advance, you will encounter unforeseen obstacles once you begin.

The best way to avoid bankruptcy is to understand why most businesses fail, and the most common reason is because their owners have cash flow problems. This simply means the money that was coming into the business did not adequately cover the money that had to be spent to run it.

Plan Your Cash Flow.

When you are making financial projections for your company, don't just make an overall plan, but itemize the cash you'll need to stay in business and where it will be coming from and when.

You must be careful to coordinate the money coming in with the money required to spend to keep your business alive. The main reason businesses fail is not because they lack adequate start-up capital but because they get caught in a cash flow crunch. The costs continued but the money simply was not coming in. For instance, if you have an office and a secretary and are in the public relations business, you have regular monthly expenses to meet. Unless your clients pay you on a monthly basis or some other agreed-upon schedule, you could be in trouble. If you have a major client who does not pay you for six months, you could be in serious trouble. How are you going to pay your secretary and the rent?

When you prepare to start a company, determining how much money you need to begin is only one factor. *Figuring how you are going to raise the money to sustain your venture should be a major consideration.* And when you estimate your future expenses, add 20 percent. Usually your expenses will be that much greater than you expect. If you have doubts about having the cash flow to keep your new company going, you would do well to find another business instead.

Undercapitalization

Capitalization, which is what accountants call having available spending money, is a frequent problem, notes accountant Ed Mendlowitz. "People sit down and in great detail they'll figure out how much they'll make or lose. They make elaborate projections. But they don't project how much cash they'll need. At the beginning stages of starting a company, *cash* is the name of the game—not profits or income." He mentions three situations that may give you cash flow problems in the initial stages:

1. Suppliers may expect cash *before delivery*—not even a C.O.D.— for a new business with no credit history.
2. Once you start production or hire employees, you'll need a regular stream of cash to meet your payroll requirements.
3. Even though you may contract to get receivables—what you are owed—within thirty days, *possibly you won't get paid for ninety days.* This can create an excruciating situation, even if you are doing well. You can't stock your inventory because of cash flow problems, and you might lose customers permanently.

Run a Tight Ship.

One entrepreneur says that because she operates a blue chip boutique she has to deliberately overstaff and spend money for elaborate presentations. Her customers expect the flash and the service she provides. She planned in advance to meet the cash flow requirements a fancy shop requires.

But for most small firms, being overstaffed can seriously drain your cash. A public relations firm owner notes: "People don't want to lay employees off when they lose accounts. You have to. I always think about who I'd fire first and who would go last. You have to be prepared. You have to adjust the overhead constantly to conform with what's coming in. If business isn't here, people go."

Charge a Fair Price.

Even the most talented women don't know how to price their services high enough. Confesses a New York attorney, "I'd do an incorporation for someone and I'd say, 'How can I charge anyone for this? It only took me ten minutes.' I'd have to force myself to charge for three hours. Women have problems in this business, charging enough for something easy. It's easier for men to say, 'Gee, I did a super job. I think I deserve a bonus of $200,000.' Most women lawyers I know won't do that. They're probably moral and right, but the men are rich and they're probably not wrong."

Prepare to Collect Promptly.

Regardless of how much you charge, you may be slow to collect. "A lot of women have a problem: they'll send the bill out, but then they don't pursue it. That really goes back to the old am-I-really-worth-it question," notes a woman who says she herself has a hard time collecting.

A woman who runs a school for adults has set up student agreement forms and incentives for paying in advance. Before, she had "terrible problems collecting." A woman in public relations says she finds it painful to pursue her slow-paying creditors. A woman in advertising says she's constantly being stretched because blue chip clients take up to six months to pay. New work keeps coming in, but the cash flow is tenuous.

If a customer is in a cash flow bind, negotiate with him. Persuade him to begin to pay you in installments, to help alleviate your own distress.

If you take on an account that will entail substantial billing, you should not hesitate to check the credit of the company or persons you are dealing with. The easiest way to investigate is to ask for a bank reference and a couple of other supplier references. The banker will tell you if the customer has a good cash flow and reserves on hand. The suppliers can tell you if the company pays promptly.

Of course, you can never be absolutely sure someone will pay you. There's a certain amount of good faith that exists between most businesses. Use your intuition here. Listen to what your "gut" tells you about the creditworthiness of a customer.

Further, if you are in a business where your customers put off paying you for three or four months, stretching out your cash reserves, negotiate with them. Give them incentives to pay promptly.

Discount 2 percent if they pay within thirty days. If your delays are really serious, discount more.

Any time you are talking with a customer about a sizable order or contract, you should discuss payment at the beginning. Don't be shy. Don't be reluctant to charge a fee that is competitive. If you are consulting on a project that is three months long, ask for an up-front payment or payment in installments. If you are catering a large event, ask for prepayment to cover your expenditures for food and beverages so that you are not put in the position of financing your patron. If you find it necessary to hire other people to complete a project, first discuss it with your client and arrange for the client to write the checks to pay them.

Prepare to Tough Out the Hard Times.

Another woman who says she is never sure where her next client is coming from is prudent with whatever cash she has on hand. She doesn't ever borrow any money—just in case it's two weeks before a new client shows up. She pays strictly as she goes.

Don't Put All Your Eggs in One Basket.

Create a financial safety net in case you should fail. Try to keep part of your assets free of your business so that if your business fails, you have something to fall back on. Don't invest everything you own in a business, and be conservative until you have a great deal of experience. Don't take out loans you could never repay should your business fail.

Strategies to Help You Run Your Business

Now that you've got your business started, you have a new series of challenges. You must direct its course so it continues to flourish and grow. You have to reward your employees and persuade them to stay with you. You should weigh the merits of incorporating and of buying various types of insurance. Most important, you have to plan your growth, progressing thoughtfully and carefully.

There is much to do once a business is under way. Choices have to be made and then continually reevaluated as the marketplace shifts and your company adjusts. A company is not a static entity like a piece of furniture that you create once, then leave alone. It is a living organization in a dynamic world. *Your ability to fine-tune it is the mark of your sensitivity and judgment.*

CHAPTER SIXTEEN

Your Employees Are the Lifeblood of Your Business: Woo Them

Your business is not merely an economic enterprise. It is also a social being, with a pulse and a heart beat that comes from you and the people you choose to work for you. It has a chemistry and a vitality that is unique.

Ultimately, your company is a reflection of your own ideas and personality, no matter how many or how few people you hire. For that reason you want to be very careful to attract the best workers and keep them with you.

After you find good employees you must engineer incentives to make them want to stay with you. But if your business is young and growing, you may simply not generate the kind of cash flow that permits you to pay them as much as they are worth. What you can do is supply perks and benefits that give them another *kind* of remuneration—hopefully to keep key employees through the early years of your company.

First Give Them Perks.

Perks are ways of making a job more attractive even when the salary is below what you would like to pay. They are one of the most cost-efficient ways of attracting and keeping the kind of employees you want.

Flexible Work Schedule—This is one of the cheapest perks there is. Letting your employees pick the hours and days that they work can mean a great deal to them, particularly if they have small children at home. "We give them more vacations and holidays," notes one designer, "and if an employee is late or takes a three-hour lunch, I look the other way."

Opportunity to Learn—If you are lucky enough to attract young, eager helpers, the opportunity to grow may be stimulating enough to compensate for a minimal salary. "I give my people responsibilities. I build confidence in them," says caterer Judith Jones. "I teach them everything I know." "I give my crew authority and responsibility," says a shop owner. "I get them directly involved in the whole operation."

Recognition—If you are outstanding at what you do, young employees want to be associated with you. Working for you provides them with an important credential to help them achieve future career goals. You may be able to attract employees for as long as a couple of years paying only minimum wages if you can add enough cachet to their portfolios.

Discounts—Giving employees a discount on any merchandise you sell is an advantage you have if you are a clothes manufacturer or retailer. Also, if you own a clothing store, permitting employees to wear your expensive clothes while they are working raises morale.

Travel—If your business is travel-related, sending an employee can provide excitement and a change of pace. For instance, Dianne

Benson, a retailer and designer, sent one of her key employees to Europe and another to Tokyo. If there is a business-related convention in an exotic locale, taking along an employee provides him/her with a break and an enhanced sense of self-worth.

Memberships—Providing a corporate membership in a country club or a fitness institute can offer employees access to places they might not otherwise be able to afford. Lillian Vernon Katz, the mail-order empress, has brought health programs into her company. She provides cancer detection, hypertension testing, and overall fitness programs for her employees.

Paid Vacations—Giving your employees paid time off is a major bonus. By permitting more vacation time than your competition, you may be able to lure talented people to you. Instead of paying a bonus, you may find it cheaper to give an employee an extra week or two of vacation that year. The reason: The salary was already budgeted for the year. Perhaps the bonus was not.

Expense Accounts—Permitting your employees to take colleagues and business associates to lunch and dinner is a valued perk. Your employees gain status in the eyes of their peers.

Credit Cards—Providing your employees with a credit card for business expenses prevents them from having to spend their own cash and avoids cash advance paperwork. Also, it is perceived by your employees as a status symbol.

Benefits Are Wonderful but Costly.

You can't consider offering benefits to employees until your company is providing sufficient cash flow for you to commit yourself to them. But once you can afford to fund benefits, you will find they promote the peace of mind and security that prompt your people to work for you as dedicated and happy employees.

One caveat to consider when you magnanimously endow your employees with a perk: It's only human nature for them to take it for granted after they've had it for a while. Benefits, once given, become the expected. You will probably find it necessary from time to time to remind employees of what the real dollar advantages are of the benefits you supply.

Health Insurance—This has become the first paid-for benefit most workers desire, particularly after they reach the age of forty. Adding dental coverage and extending the coverage to include the spouses and offspring of your employees can win you loyalty.

Life Insurance—Group term life insurance policies for your employees up to $50,000 per person can be paid for by your company tax free. The only drawback is that if you buy life insurance for one employee, you are required to provide for them all.

Profit Sharing—A profit-sharing plan makes sense *after* your company is generating a healthy profit. In profit-sharing plans, a percentage of the profits are set aside for all the employees of the company. If you set up a fund and accrue the money for them, the employees know they have a nest egg and are also sharing in the profits. Knowing they benefit from the company's success both motivates your people and builds morale.

You only have to contribute to a profit-sharing plan if you make a profit. If you don't make money in a given year, you don't have to pay into the fund.

Profit sharing does have its downside. If you are having a streak of bad luck and there are no profits, key employees can become disenchanted and quit. When they leave, if they are "vested"— qualified for their rights to the money in the fund—they get to take their money, or a percentage of their money, with them.

One nice note on profit sharing: These plans are the most beneficial to you as the owner of your company; they are geared to pay based on salary, and yours will likely be the highest.

Pension Plans—A pension plan is desirable once your company is operating smoothly, because it provides security for your employees—a plus if they are forty-five or over.

However, you will be the greatest beneficiary of a pension plan, because your share of the money will be based on salary, and after your company is thriving, your own salary is far higher than that of your employees.

Ed Mendlowitz, a New York accountant, favors pension plans because he views them as tax shelters. In a pension plan compensation is deducted by the company and saved for employees to produce earnings that gain interest over the years. Neither the original amount set aside nor the amount earned is taxed until you draw money, but when you retire you will probably be in a lower tax bracket. Mendlowitz thinks pension funds are particularly attractive for business owners. You get to save money that otherwise would have been taxed as part of your profit.

Pension plans should qualify under the complicated rules of the Employee Retirement Income Security Act (ERISA). The rules are cumbersome. You'll have to consult an accountant.

You should note that a pension plan, once begun, must be contributed to every year according to the formula you have decided upon. Even if you have a loss, you have to contribute.

There is a simpler kind of pension fund designed to avoid some of the complicated paperwork required by ERISA in the usual fund. In it you contribute directly into your employees' Individual Retirement Account (IRA). It is simple, but it is also inflexible. It is not the ideal employment incentive package. Any time employees quit, the IRA is still theirs.

A pension plan is not something you want to put into place before your company is in a strong financial position. "We deferred all our pension plans, thrift plans, and employee benefits," notes Anita Miller, who founded the AmeriFederal Savings Bank in 1984. "We can always add the benefits."

Employee Stock Ownership Plan (ESOP)—This is a pension or profit-sharing plan that allows your employees to buy stock in your company. This way they not only have a plan, they also have stock in the company. Once again there are rules about how long employees have to work for you before the stock is theirs outright.

ESOPs are really only feasible for companies earning more than $100,000 in profits *before taxes*. Like the other employee benefit programs, it is complicated and you will need an expert accountant.

Stock Ownership—Key employees will likely ask you for a piece of the action. If your company prospers, they may want a percentage of the operation. One way to divide your company into pieces is to issue stock, assuming that you are incorporated. While this may provide the employee with a sense of participation, a minority holding gives them no control and few added rights.

The most important thing to consider when you think about offering shares is how you're going to buy them back when the employee leaves. You want an ironclad buy-back contract that goes with the stock, permitting you to recover the shares at a price determined by a formula you work out *before* you let any stock out of your hands.

Think at least a thousand times before you decide to issue pieces of your company. Usually, a key employee who gets 3 percent will be back on your doorstep the following year asking for more. If your company is successful, some of your people are always going to want more. You must decide the limits to which you are willing to be pushed. After you become a successful entrepreneur, your employees tend to forget the skill, work, luck, and risks you experienced on your way to success.

Annual Bonuses— This is a windfall for the employee the first time. After that it becomes preplanned as part of their salary. A bonus is most effective if it is paid out randomly without prior notice as a reward for work recently completed.

Special Benefits You Can Supply When You've Got Lots of Cash.

Once your company is established and has a long record of financial success, there are other generous benefits you can extend to your treasured employees.

Salary After Retirement—If employees serve you for many years, you can reward them after they have retired by paying them a salary that combined with their pensions enables them to have the same level of income they enjoyed while they were working for you.

Continued Employment—One generous benefit you can offer people who work for you for many years is to permit them never to retire, letting them work as much as they like as long as they like. You continue to pay them their usual full-time salary. For people who live for their jobs, this is a humane and life-prolonging benefit.

Deferred Compensation—If you and your key employees build such a successful company that you are making more money than you need, you can arrange for deferred compensation. You enter into a contract arranging for some of your compensation to be paid to you or your employees at a future date. The money will not be taxed until it is paid out.

Salary Boosts—Once your company is well entrenched, you can afford to pay extravagant salaries to key employees. But take heed: money itself is not enough to motivate employees. You still need to go out of your way to let them know you value them. You need to *nurture* them to *motivate* them to work at their highest level of productivity.

Provide Challenges for Your Employees.

Giving perks and benefits to your employees is important, but not sufficient to motivate them to perform to the best of their ability.

The most effective way to keep the best employees is to *provide them with challenges*. If you've hired the right people, expanding their responsibilities will enable them to grow on the job. There is a thrill and a gratification that comes from meeting challenges and learning. When you can guide your employees in this direction, they will feel enormous satisfaction about their accomplishments.

Once they begin to grow and meet challenges, you have to continue to feed them new ones. Some people thrive on the discipline required to expand their capabilities. When opportunities to surmount new hurdles diminish, your highest-achieving employees may become bored.

Communicate with Your People.

You rely on your employees, and it is critical that they have a clear understanding of exactly what you want to accomplish with your business. They need to understand your goals and pull in the same direction with you. It is up to you to provide them with a definite sense of your objectives.

Frequently, particularly if your business is small and you are scrambling, you may neglect your internal communications. Don't. It's good for employee morale when your staff understands where you are going.

One important advantage of constant communication is that danger signals are less likely to be ignored. In an open environment your employees will be more inclined to alert you to the slightest prospect of something running amok in order to give you time to avoid it.

You should schedule regular meetings, probably weekly, to review work in progress and discuss new business. The effectiveness of these meetings is a responsibility that falls on your shoulders. You should prepare an agenda. At the meetings you should deal promptly with the items on the agenda. You should create an atmosphere where your employees feel free to disagree or make suggestions.

If you involve your key staff members in your planning sessions, you may find they have ideas that are valuable to the progress of your company. Reward them. Implement their ideas. Don't feel threatened if they sometimes have better ideas than you do.

Working Conditions Are Important.

Try to provide conditions conducive to getting work done. If you don't have much money and your offices are grim, promise your employees an improvement. Give them hope while they endure cramped or inappropriate quarters. Have a targeted date for a move or expansion. Show concern about any discomfort they experience. Just showing that you care makes them feel better.

But far more important than the physical environment are the psychological conditions your employees experience. High morale can offset the bleakest of working conditions.

Morale is not a constant. It changes every day. *Be sensitive to the morale in your office. When you sense it is low, give it a boost*.

One of the greatest influences on your office's morale is your own. Are you "up"? You have a profound effect on the people who work for you. Be positive. Don't permit your own frustration or discouragement to pull your employees down.

Let your employees know what reactions to expect from you. Be predictable, consistent. It makes them feel more secure.

Fire the Losers.

There is such a thing as good chemistry or "good vibrations." You can feel it. Bad chemistry in your office is trouble. A sour, negative person can spoil a barrel of apples. Don't tolerate "an attitude." Fire that person quickly. The longer a troublemaker is in your office, the more disruptive it will be.

If you have an employee who goofs off or does not carry his or her full load, that person can undermine the morale of the other hardworking employees. Take immediate action. Tell the shirker to shape up or ship out. If you fail to act, you have signaled that underperformance is tolerated. Overachievers will become disgruntled.

Firing is a miserable experience, but a necessary one. You cannot tolerate or afford incompetence.

Danger Signals That You Are Not Delegating Properly.

You are irritable and overworked all of the time. You can't do everything yourself. Delegate the tasks someone else can do and focus on what you do best.

You procrastinate so long it is a problem for your business. Hire someone to do tasks you dislike. Save your high energy for the parts of the business you enjoy the most.

Your open door policy is getting out of hand. Your employees take up all of your time at the office. Delegate employee relations to someone and concentrate on making yourself available only on key issues. Don't get so involved with the personal lives of your underlings that it hampers your performance.

You feel tired and depressed when you get up in the morning. You dread facing your office. You may be overworked because you are trying to carry too much of the load. Allocate several of your most grueling tasks to employees who can handle them.

You neglect your clients because the office work is up to your ears. Bring in an office manager. Delegate. Don't let anything distract you from the mainstream of your business.

You sense a morale problem among your employees. Investigate to see if it stems from overwork or a lack of understanding of their functions. Good delegating includes explaining to employees the importance or significance of their tasks.

Tasks often are not done correctly by your employees and you have to work until midnight to straighten them out. Are you explaining the tasks correctly? If repeated errors occur, either you have the wrong employee, you are unable to adequately communicate the job at hand, or you do not have sufficient checks and balances for the employee to evaluate his/her accuracy.

Your secretary gets so overworked she gets mononucleosis. You should hire an assistant for her or an assistant for yourself.

Key employees quit because they feel frustrated about the lack of responsibility they were given. You have to give people enough authority to be able to carry out tasks. This also means they will have the freedom to fail. Try to check their progress often enough to avoid failures, but not so much as to make them feel stifled. If you have good, capable employees, use them.

Your employees continually fail to produce at the rate you expect. Either the work load is too great or you have the wrong employees.

CHAPTER SEVENTEEN

You Can Hire
Your Family

If you own your own company, you are in charge of your corporate policy toward your family members. You are free to integrate your husband, mother, and children into the business to the extent that you choose. The options are all yours. You're the boss. You write the rules. Your entire family may be in the business, as is the case with Jeanne Kennedy. She has six Meineke Discount Muffler franchises in Houston, Texas. Her two daughters, one son, one son-in-law, and her husband all work in the franchise businesses. "As we expanded we decided to get the rest of the family in the business," declares Kennedy.

You Can Hire Your Children.

"We believe in nepotism," declares Beverly Garland, who owns the Beverly Garland Howard Johnson in Hollywood, California.

Two children and a granddaughter of Garland, who plays Kate Jackson's mother in the TV show *The Scarecrow & Mrs. King*, work at the hotel she owns. A son runs a Sacramento hotel owned by Garland and her husband.

It is perfectly acceptable to hire your own children if they are qualified for the job. Mary Kay Ash's son Richard Rogers is president of Mary Kay Cosmetics. Both of Lillian Vernon Katz's sons work for Lillian Vernon. Georgette Klinger's daughter, Kathryn, is the president of the chain bearing her mother's name.

Hiring Your Children Can Have Drawbacks.

If you are in partnership with someone, hiring your children can be a more complicated concern. The family of the other partner has to be considered.

By the same token, however, you cannot hire family members to reap all the benefits without also being sensitive to the reactions of your other employees. Lynn Wilson's interior design firm hires talented and highly skilled people who work together as a team. She deliberately has *not* employed her family members because she thinks the other employees might resent seeing the benefits accrue to her own family unit. "My son works for us during the summer and that's it," comments Wilson. "The other employees might resent it because the profits are supposed to flow to them."

Hiring Several Family Members Takes Advance Planning.

Should several children join your company, you must plan for the fact that only one chief executive officer can succeed you. The children must be prepared from the beginning to work as a team, deferring to the designated successor to the front office or running the firm jointly as partners. Harriet Gerber Lewis of Gerber Plumbing Fixtures, which was founded by her father, ran the Illinois-based manufacturing company in equal partnership with her brother for many years.

After her brother's death, Lewis became president. Gerber, which manufactures a broad line of plumbing fixtures, has been in business for over fifty years. A third generation of family management is in place to succeed Lewis. She notes, "You don't just take family members in, pat them on the back and say, 'Oh, you're doing a great job.' You don't take them on and call them a vice-president right off. They have to prove themselves."

Your Business Can Provide a Career Option for Your Husband.

You might opt to start your business while your husband holds down another job. Then, after your company gets going, he can exercise the option of joining your already thriving enterprise. Such was the case with Barbara Rowan of Rowan Associates, a firm specializing in investigating corporate fraud. Her husband, who was a seasoned member of the FBI, is a perfect adjunct to her own efforts.

Dot Carswell, who owns a Century 21 franchise in New Jersey, notes that when her husband retired as an executive in a large corporation, he joined her to handle some of the operations. The husband of Barbara Einbinder, another Century 21 franchisee, also opted to come into her business. "I guess my success gave him an opportunity to change careers," notes Einbinder.

Frequently husband/wife teams in business make for very successful relationships. Barriers between work and private life frequently disappear as a day at the vacation house affords an opportunity to hash out problems. These relationships are intense and satisfying on several levels.

There Can Be Tax Advantages in Hiring Your Spouse.

There are good tax incentives to consider putting your husband on the payroll if your company is thriving.

One has to do with deducting travel expenses for your husband when he accompanies you on business trips. The Internal Revenue Service is taking an increasingly dim view of claiming that your husband is a business entertainment asset, making it difficult to justify deducting his travel and hotel expenses. But if your husband is on your payroll and performs specific services for your company, the entire matter is much simpler. All you have to do, when challenged by the IRS, is explain the genuine business reason your husband was present. However, if he's on the payroll, you are far less likely to be challenged in the first place.

You also get a tax break if your husband is studying career-related educational courses. You can deduct any tuition costs for courses that improve his job skills.

A major benefit of hiring your husband and putting him on the payroll is that he can receive pension and profit-sharing benefits if your business is thriving. Further, paying two generous salaries is an excellent way for you to take cash out of the company as it grows.

Of course, your husband has to really perform duties at the company. Moreover, he should draw a salary that is in line with the area of the country where you live and what other people in the same business are earning. Further, you should keep records to document that he is a real employee, performs duties, and shows up. If you are challenged, your records may save the day.

CHAPTER EIGHTEEN

How You Structure Your Company Is Important

It is tempting to get caught up in the day-to-day stream of business and put off making decisions about some of the details, such as exactly what kind of structure is best for you or what kind of insurance you need.

But these little details can have important financial ramifications to your ultimate success. After your business has gotten going, you should take the time to examine the options available.

Should You Incorporate?

The main reason you should incorporate is to protect yourself from personal liability. If you fail in business or are the subject of a major lawsuit, only the money in that business is at stake. Your car, your future earnings, and your savings and your jewelry—any personal assets you have—are not affected. What's more, you are not responsible for the company. The company is only responsible for itself. Its debts and its problems are legally separate from you.

When you incorporate you create a separate entity, a company apart from you. You work for it. It pays you a salary. It has a bank account. It has a separate relationship with Uncle Sam. This is different from a proprietorship, any unincorporated business, where your own life and the business you do are mixed up together.

A corporation has a life of its own. You can think of it as a guard standing between you and customers protecting you from being personally liable for any debts or judgments against your business. If you are an unincorporated caterer and a customer gets sick from one of your cakes and sues you, are are personally liable for his lawsuit. If you are incorporated, the sick customer sues your company. Your company is liable only to the extent that it has assets. You and all your personal possessions are free and clear.

Another advantage of incorporating is that you establish shares of stock as part of the process of incorporation. These shares are easily transferrable when you want to sell all or part of your business.

The entity you create has yet another advantage for you: it never dies or retires. It just goes on and on, unless deliberate steps are made to bring it to an end. Should you die or retire, your company still exists. This gives continuity to your business, which makes succession easier for your designated heirs.

Moreover, incorporating provides an opportunity for you to provide retirement health benefits for yourself. Only when you incorporate are these benefits tax free. Incorporated, you can provide life, sickness, and disability insurance with pretax dollars. Unincorporated, you pay for these things with after-tax dollars.

There is only one disadvantage to incorporating and that is a consideration only if you are very successful. After you have provided handsomely for your employees and yourself, paid yourself a wonderful salary, and accumulated profits of over $150,000 after taxes, which just sit in the company, Uncle Sam gets greedy. He tries to force you to pay dividends so that he can collect taxes twice: dividends are paid out of *after-tax* corporate profits, but the recipient has to pay taxes on them as well. The biggest cat-and-mouse game in history is the one in which corporations scheme and plot how to outsmart Uncle Sam and avoid paying those doubly taxed dividends. You can either expand to avoid retaining so much cash, or you can use some of the money to hire the best accountants in town to help you devise truly creative bookkeeping techniques. Such are the problems of success.

When Should You Not Incorporate?

If you are under twenty-years of age, most states will not permit you to incorporate.

If you make $20,000 a year and you work in an area where there is no personal liability, you don't have to incorporate, particularly if you are young and healthy and feel you can get by without health benefits. For instance, if you are a designer, you have no personal liability. On the other hand, if you are a caterer and your client gets food poisoning you are vulnerable to a lawsuit unless you incorporate.

However, you should not incorporate if it is inconceivable that you could maintain records and handle detailed paperwork. A certain amount of care is necessary to sustain the paper entity you have created.

How to Begin.

The first thing to do when you decide to incorporate is to pick a name for your company, since the forms you will have to fill out require this. You should choose several different names and then send them listed in the order of your preference, with a letter indicating your intentions, to your local secretary of state. This allows you to see if one of those names is available. You can't use a name if someone else has already chosen it. Moreover, some states have a list of taboo names that can't be used in corporation titles, such as "bond" in New York State.

When a name is free, you then must indicate that you want it reserved for your use. Generally, a name will be held for a couple of months. You have to use Inc. or Corp. or Ltd. in the name of your company once you incorporate: you are required by law to indicate that you have a legal status for your business.

Choosing names is frequently a source of great deliberation. Your name should be applicable to your company. Creating one isn't always easy.

You may pick a name because it's memorable. Elizabeth Woolf picked the name Renta Yenta even though she didn't like it. "I hate it, but it's catchy. It's narrow in its definition. People don't forget it, that's the magic of it." Woolf's company provides a variety of services, from picking up someone at the airport to personal shopping.

You can name your business after yourself. Susan Bang named her company Bang Communications. "It's personal," she explains. But naming a company after yourself can have disadvantages. Lynn Wilson, who has an interior design firm in Coral Gables, Florida, originally named her business Lynn Wilson Associates. But she changed it to Creative Environs to put herself in the background and emphasize the team approach she uses. "If you want to keep people, you have to motivate them, make them feel like a part of the business."

Debbie Storrs deliberately named her collection company after herself, but she calls it D. Storrs & Associates, Inc. She figured that since the business is typically male-dominated, not identifying herself as "Debbie" might be a positive move.

If you expect to be very successful, you may opt to name your company after something besides yourself so that if you decide to sell, your name is not part of the package. That's what Sandy Shutak did. She named her company CCI Communications. "It could mean anything," notes Shutak. The initials stand for nothing in particular.

Decide on a Fiscal Year.

A fiscal year doesn't have to begin on January 1 and end on December 31. You can choose any beginning date and your fiscal year ends a year later. The U.S. government's fiscal year, for instance, begins October 1 and ends September 30.

The simplest fiscal year is a calendar year. If you have a simple business, take the simple solution. But accountant Ed Mendlowitz suggests that if your business is larger and more complicated, you might consider picking another fiscal year.

In a seasonal business, he notes, the fiscal year should never end after the busy season, but after the slow one instead. Your income peaks give you strength to draw against during the subsequent slower season, and you reap the tax benefits from your losses immediately, because your year closes immediately after your nadir.

Moreover, having a strong first quarter in your fiscal year can help you with the banks, giving you a psychological boost with your banker. If the first half of your fiscal year were your slow season, your banker could take a wait-and-see attitude and delay a loan until the end of your fiscal year.

How to Incorporate.

To incorporate you apply for two documents. From the Internal Revenue Service you apply for an employer identification number. This is like the Social Security number of the fictitious person you are inventing; it is used at banks to open corporate accounts and on other forms you send to state and national agencies. Then you buy a certificate of incorporation at an office supply store, fill it out, and send it to the state capitol. They send you back a corporate seal, which is the "signature" of your fictitious person.

Your company must adhere to the various procedures your particular state requires for incorporated firms. You have to keep records; regardless of the size of your business, the rules apply. You have to have regular meetings of your board of directors—family and friends can be named—and minutes of the meetings must be kept.

The way you dissolve a corporation is very much like the way you start it—legally canceling its existence with the state.

Should You Form a Subchapter S Corporation?

The name refers to the subchapter S in the Internal Revenue Code. A subchapter S is more technically complicated than a basic corporation, but it permits you to avoid some of the problems of success mentioned earlier.

With the subchapter S corporation you create a separate entity that protects you personally against liabilities of doing business. But the operation's earnings or losses don't stay in the company. They pass through directly to you.

This "pass through" is what makes the complicated subchapter S so appealing. It is often used by affluent individuals who are starting up a business that is going to lose money initially. For instance, if you are starting a production company and you need to buy new equipment and a factory, you would form a subchapter S and then use the losses and tax credits against your personal income to reduce your personal taxes.

The subchapter S is ideal for absorbing early losses because it is easy to turn the corporation into an ordinary one at will. Thus you might form a subchapter S company when you first open your manufacturing business and use the losses to reduce your own tax bill; then, when your business becomes profitable, you could turn the corporation into a regular one and let the earnings be used to run the business.

The rules for maintaining a subchapter S are complex. Unless you follow them meticulously you can endanger the special status the company gives you.

Lynn Wilson, who founded Creative Environs, says she started out as a subchapter S corporation "for liability security and tax reasons." She reports, "It was very limiting, but it made sense because I was small. After three years I changed to a standard corporation because I was making too much money."

The ideal subchapter S businesses are those in which start-up costs are high and no profitability is expected for a couple of years, such as a sportswear concern that buys the machinery to produce the clothes or a construction company that buys bulldozers and cranes.

What Kind of Insurance Do You Need?

Incorporation in itself is an insurance policy. The mere act of formalizing your company insures you from being vulnerable to potentially devastating liabilities.

It is important to note that once you are incorporated you can provide yourself with disability and life insurance. As an employee of your own company, you can be insured with workmen's compensation insurance. It is paid for with pretax dollars of your corporation and is a tax-deductible item. This in itself is motivation for some solo entrepreneurs to incorporate.

You also need regular business insurance to protect yourself against loss, theft, or damage of office equipment and inventory. Be sure you also cover inventory in transit. Usually you take responsibility for inventory when it leaves the warehouse, not when it arrives at your store. You may also need insurance to protect you against errors and omissions, such as malpractice insurance.

Shop around before you buy insurance. Find out what different kinds of deals agents and insurance companies can give you. Look for both quality and economy. Every few years, shop around again.

Don't let the fine print overwhelm you. Ask specific questions. Don't be afraid to admit you don't understand something. Let your potential agents earn their commissions by providing you with service—the service of educating you.

Moreover, you shouldn't assume you automatically buy all your insurance from a single agent. Accept separate business coverage and life insurance bids.

CHAPTER NINETEEN

Growth Must Be Carefully Planned

There is nothing magic about growth. It is not an assurance that you will be successful or that your business is in good shape. Growing carries with it results you should weigh carefully.

Growth of your company means added responsibilities for you. It means you have more customers to please, more employees to hire, and more administrative work to do. Your growth could mean you'll require a larger space to work in, which could also mean an expensive move and more desks and telephones.

Most important, your growth should be in the right place—the bottom line. When your company grows, profits must also keep pace to make it worth your time and effort. Don't ever forget that a small, profitable company makes a lot more sense than a large, unprofitable, or marginally profitable, undertaking. What is the point of expanding your company's business to $1 million a year with profits of $100,000 if on revenues of $500,000 you still make a profit of $100,000? You've increased the headaches and responsibilities of the business without adding a cent to the bottom line. It isn't worth the bother.

How to Plan Your Growth.

The most successful growth is meticulously planned. Flourishing businesses are run by people who have an intuitive sense of how much they can handle, how much growth they can accommodate without losing control. It is important to understand exactly how much your organization can absorb without being overwhelmed. It is essential that you understand the limitations of your company and yourself and always keep your growth within these limits.

The easiest way to grow is to start small and progress one step at a time. "You should begin small and grow. Your skills develop as your responsibilities expand," advises Deborah Szekely, who expanded the Golden Door. "Start small and learn. You can grow later."

Mary Kay Cosmetics is an example of starting small and growing systematically. Mary Kay Ash first opened a modest cosmetics store in 1963 next door to a coffee shop in an office building, hoping the women who worked in the building would stop on their way to lunch or coffee. They did. "Six months later we were working until three in the morning filling orders," she recalls. "In nine months we moved into our first office building."

Ash continued to grow a step at a time over a twenty-year period. Mary Kay Cosmetics employs almost 200,000 salespeople. Sales are over $300 million annually.

Before you even consider expanding your business, you should sit down and project exactly how much profit you will make from future growth. Include several "what ifs" in your figures; for example, what if a department store wants one thousand cakes in December—could you handle the order, and would it be profitable? Think your business through carefully. If you have given it thought in advance, you won't be caught off guard when the unexpected occurs. You'll be ready to spring into action.

Having preplanned your company's growth leaves you freer to cope with the nitty-gritty of rapid success. This is important, because growing means many hectic moments, as attested to by Debbie Storrs. "It's out of hand now. We are divisionalizing the collection business right now and moving around accountants and changing collectors. It's mass confusion," Storrs reports cheerfully. "You can lay the best business plan, but when you grow, something is always slipping through the cracks."

Some Growth Comes Naturally.

It's easiest to grow if your business is in a market that is growing. Anita Jacobson, owner of Alitta, which manufactures sportswear for bicyclists, expects to grow because bicycling is increasingly popular: "I've done my market research. I'm on a crest now in positioning and timing. I saw it coming with the cycle marathons, the triathalons," she reports.

If you're in a booming market, the momentum can carry you over some rough spots. For instance, the bicycling miniboom was a big help to Jacobson, whose background is in philosophy and business—not in design. She advises, "The timing and the market have been so right on that they've carried me through some of the mistakes I probably would not have made if I'd had design experience."

Recognize the Limits to Your Business.

Don't get carried away with the idea of growth for the sake of growth. Don't kid yourself about what your customers expect. If it's the personal touch that has made you successful, don't grow so big you risk losing it. Lynn Wilson realizes that Creative Environs, her firm, is about as big as she should let it get for that very reason. "Having twenty-three employees is a number I think I can handle and still have a personal touch," she comments. "I don't want to lose the very thing that made me a success."

By the same token, if you own one restaurant that's immensely successful, don't have illusions about opening two or three. Maybe you can't duplicate the magic you created in one place. Such is the case of Faith Stewart-Gordon, owner of the Russian Tea Room, a perennially popular New York establishment. She says, "We're working on merchandizing some of our products and we'll expand our space within this building, but not to have another restaurant. I just don't think it would work. It wouldn't be the same. And if it did work, it wouldn't have the touch."

In some industries survival depends on the flexibility that only a small business can maintain. Such is the case of Myrtle Willey's company, T. W. Dick, a Maine-based steel producer. "It's easier to cope with the constant change in the steel business by staying small," says Willey. "I've watched some of my peers grow and I've watched their problems grow. Bigger is not necessarily better. It's not worth all the headaches when you start reaching out."

You Don't Have to Grow Big.

Stories of rapid and extensive growth are impressive, but growing a big company is not the right thing for everyone. Many entrepreneurs find as much satisfaction in running a prospering small business. Letitia Baldrige, for instance, after serving as chief of staff to Jacqueline Onassis when she was the nation's first lady, no doubt could have built as large a public relations business as she wanted. But she preferred a small, personal company with only nine employees working for her. Comments Baldrige, "I didn't want to be any bigger. I wanted a nice income and freedom and the total creative life—not having to wrestle with administrative problems."

She continues, "I've run large staffs—five hundred people—but I'd rather be at the core of the business, working one to one with a chief executive. I do a lot of consulting and would rather spend those two hours with the CEO than have to go back and face a sea of a thousand people in my shop and know that the vice-president of human resources is waiting for me. With some women being small is just a matter of choice." Don't be trapped into believing you have to be big to be a success. Success is being able to be anything you decide to be.

Expanding Your Facilities.

There seems to be an unwritten rule that you outgrow your business facility and work in miserably cramped quarters before you move to larger, more spacious quarters. Then they, too, one day become miserable and cramped, if you are growing, and you have to move again.

Getting out of one lease and entering another is a hassle, and moves are expensive. The ideal way to expand is to locate some place where your growth can be handled without the trauma of major relocation.

The story of the late Bette Nesmith Graham's Liquid Paper company exemplifies the ideal of spatial flexibility to accommodate growth. Nesmith Graham started out in her one-car garage in 1960 making up five-gallon batches of the typing correction fluid and filling bottles of Liquid Paper from ketchup squeeze bottles. Soon five thousand bottles a week were being produced.

Then Nesmith Graham erected a small portable building in her backyard, and later another. As sales burgeoned, Nesmith Graham kept adding portable buildings until she had seven. They made for a strange sight: one truck driver who was trying to make a delivery mistakingly assumed the company for one in the portable building business.

It was not until the company had developed a steadily growing, stable business in 1968 that Nesmith Graham committed company resources to a traditional manufacturing facility.

It is probably unlikely you could erect a temporary building in your backyard to house your business, but the moral of the Nesmith Graham story should not be overlooked: Start simply and build slowly. Start in your house and expand to your garage. The fancy digs can come later, after you have solid, substantial business. Don't overrate the importance of your image when the most important thing is to perform with excellence and remain in business.

You Can Grow Through Diversification.

One way to grow is to diversify your product line. For instance, Bettye Martin, the head of Gear, entered the home furnishings marketplace with a country look called "Country Gear." It was a great success. Lest the look prove to be only a fad, Martin brought out two different looks. City Dimensionals is a modern and very contemporary line that appeals to those who don't buy the country style. New Traditionalists, a style that blends French and English antiques with elegant fabrics and contemporary accents, is aimed at the more affluent end of the market.

You can diversify the range of services you offer. Anne Ready, whose media consulting firm in Los Angeles is a big success today, began in media training and expanded to include video sales training.

You will probably discover as you diversify that one opportunity often leads to another. Such was the case of Ann Clark, owner of LaBonne Cuisine, a cooking school in Austin, Texas, when she first diversified into catering. Eventually she began giving catering seminars for other cooking schools around the country. She also consults with restaurants about their menus, advising the chefs and the crew. Moreover, she occasionally arranges "very private, very personal trips" of small groups of people to the French countryside, visiting both friends and favorite small restaurants and inns.

When you diversify, you should never move too far afield from your main thrust of business. Look for closely related areas to move into. For instance, Rose Nemeth, a California realtor, found that the popular vacation area where she operates had a real need for rentals and rental property management. Nemeth quickly moved to offer those services.

Another example of taking related opportunities is Debbie Storrs, who opened other companies in collection agency–related areas. One sells software she developed to computerize her business. Yet another company runs training seminars for employees in the collection departments of other companies. Then, since collection agencies often have to track down scofflaws, Storrs started a business that simply helps locate people.

Computers Can Help Your Growth.

You should automatically include a computer in your operations to facilitate your growth. A realtor with a diversified business uses one to issue monthly statements and coordinate many of her operations. "I have mixed emotions about my computer," she confides. "I feel like I'm losing control."

If you have a resistance to computers, you must actively try to overcome it. The easiest way is to enroll in computer courses in the evenings. Computers can be complicated, there is no doubt about that, so give yourself a reasonable time frame, such as six months, to feel at home with one. The more you know about them, the less you will fear them. You cannot underestimate their importance.

"I think computers are absolutely essential for gaining control of your finances and business accounts," observes entrepreneur Carol Green. "You save money by having computers. You don't make as many mistakes, and mistakes cost money. Mistakes also cost you professionalism."

Personal Growth Is Important, Too.

Sometimes you might decide that your own personal growth and diversification are more important than expanding your business.

Deborah Szekely, owner of both Rancho La Puerta and the Golden Door health resort, says, "Now I'm looking for challenge, not money and not power. When I turned sixty I spent several months thinking, 'Now what can I do of all the things I've always wanted to do?' I totally changed my life." Szekely accepted a position as president of Inter-America Foundation in Washington, D.C., which has an annual budget of $25 million and funds development projects in Latin America. It is a job she sought through a recruiting company and got. She left her San Diego house for the first nine-to-five job she has ever held in her life. More personal growth lies ahead: "I thought I might go to filmmaking school at UCLA or USC when I'm seventy," she says with a smile.

When you think about expanding your company, do not forget about your own personal growth. Use the freedom of being an entrepreneur as an opportunity to focus on what pleases you most. If it is building a billion-dollar empire, by all means do it, as did Debbie Storrs, who at age thirty-two has already amassed a multi-million-dollar empire. But Storrs still has her own well-being very much in mind. "My philosophy is to achieve any kind of growth that is possible that will let me reach my goal to retire when I'm thirty-five. When I was twenty-five I agreed to bust my ass for ten years, and give up all my social life and work. I'm divorced. I don't know a man in his right mind who would put up with my kind of schedule.

"When I retire I plan to live on a sixty-foot yacht with massive computer equipment and a helicopter pad so that I can run the companies from there. I'll stay there half of the year and I'll spend the other half at some remote home in the Colorado mountains."

But if you are not willing to give up a decade of your life to achieve great success in the financial world, there is nothing wrong with you. The point of owning your own business is that you can be anything you decide you want to become. You set your own goals. You are in charge of your own life.

Advantages of Being Small

Fewer employee problems.

More intimate contact with customers.

The office has a less structured, "family" feeling.

Less administrative work.

Flexibility about the work you accept.

Flexibility about your personal work schedule.

Flexibility for your employees.

Lower overhead.

You have personal control over the work your company does.

You are personally involved with more aspects of the work.

Advantages of Being Big

You can delegate work you do not like.

You can pay yourself a bigger salary and provide perks and benefits for yourself and your people.

It is easy to get your banker's attention.

Community recognition.

You are taken seriously.

You can provide jobs for your family and others you want to assist.

You can hire experts to perform specialized tasks.

You can provide many more services for your customers.

The office has a serious, big-company feeling.

You can take long vacations and the company runs without you.

CHAPTER TWENTY

How to Find Good Advisors

Your choice of experts from the outside can be critical in the success of your venture. A clever accountant can save you thousands—or millions. A good attorney can help you protect yourself and avoid expensive litigation. A good computer consultant can implement systems that increase your company's productivity and cut down on clerical staff. An inventive interior designer can provide a more productive office arrangement.

The advisors with whom you will have the longest working relationships are your accountants and attorneys. It is especially important that the ones you choose be perfect adjuncts to your business.

Ineptitude exists in every profession. That is why it is essential you take the time to find proven, reliable advisors. If you get advice that doesn't make sense to you, double-check with another advisor. Most important, don't ever let professional advice interfere with your own good common sense.

What to Expect from Your Accountant and Attorney.

While advisors you bring in from time to time may give you only specialized, nitty-gritty information, you need more than that from your accountant and attorney. You want them to give you an overview of your business and to take a long-term perspective that includes your company's growth and development. Your associations with them will influence many of the business decisions you make.

Accessibility: Your advisors should quickly return your phone calls and research issues they are unsure of. If you are undergoing difficulties, they should make themselves particularly available to you. They should "be there." You never should be left in the lurch because you cannot get a response from your hired expert.

As your company grows, your needs may grow. Says Patricia Duncanson, head of Duncanson Electric Company, "I need someone at my beck and call to help with strategic planning, someone on a retainer. I don't just want someone to tell me what has happened after it is over. I don't need to read yesterday's newspapers. I need someone to forecast."

You have a right to make demands when you hire advisors, the same way your clients make demands on you. If you only have routine matters to cover, do not demand the same kind of accessibility as when you have major problems. However, should your advisors become lax and less accessible over the years, be firm and reiterate your expectations. If your advisors continue to fail to measure up, find new ones.

Promptness: Reports and research should be prepared in a reasonable amount of time. All deadlines your advisors set for themselves should be met.

Knowledge: If your advisor does not know and cannot quickly find out, he or she should refer to someone who does. Moreover, your advisors should keep up with all the latest developments in their areas of expertise so that the information they give you reflects all the latest rulings. If changes, such as in tax laws or legal accountability, directly affect your business decisions, your advisors should voluntarily bring you up-to-date with a prompt phone call or a letter.

Steadfastness: If you get into legal or financial problems, you surely do not want advisors who flee in the face of adversity. If you are audited, you want your accountant to represent you to the IRS. If you are sued, you want your attorney to be prepared to defend you.

Simplicity: Your advisors should give you the kind of information that helps you organize your business better. Your accountant should help you streamline your accounting system. By the same token, your attorney should help you standardize your contracts.

Good accounting and legal advice should be worth their cost to you. However, if you think your advisors are overpriced, shop around for new ones. Whenever you feel you are not getting enough assistance and information from them to justify their fees, you probably have the wrong advisors.

Good Advisors Are Not Necessarily Easy to Find.

The best way to find the right advisors is to actively go shopping for them. It is important that you find those professionals who are already thoroughly familiar with your field. If you are an artist, ask other artists and dealers. If you are a retailer, ask other retailers where they find advice. If you are opening a franchise, find advisors who routinely deal with franchisees.

Each business has its own subtleties, and if your advisors are thoroughly familiar with your particular business, they will be better prepared to inform you of the tax deductions you can take in your business or to help you avoid legal pitfalls. In short, if you run a ballet studio, do not hire an accountant who has only worked with manufacturing companies.

Use your associations and peer networks to provide information about good advisors. When you go to a trade association meeting for your business, ask several successful members who they use and if they are satisfied. When you get a name, call around to other lawyers and accountants you may know and check the reputation. When they recommend the advisor, ask what they base their approval on. Check with state associations to assure the candidate's credentials are in order.

Finding specialists in your particular field is harder if you are located in a small town. It is worth a trip to a neighboring city to get expert counsel. Just be sure the big city is in the same state, since state laws about taxes and legalities vary. Even if your advisors are not located at your back door, you will find that the telephone and mail service can provide the necessary avenues for funneling day-to-day information. Moreover, you may use big-city advisors for an overview of your situation and use a local generalist to handle some of the more mundane aspects of your services.

Do not forget you are looking for smart, crafty, sage advice. You should not settle for someone who has the right credentials but has no imagination or creativity. Persevere in your quest for the best.

Interview Them.

Make at least three interview appointments with three different advisors in the same field before you meet with the first one: this is a psychological ploy that forces you not to go with the first one you meet until you have talked to the other two.

Be up front. Say, "I'm shopping around." You should not be charged for that visit. If you are, it may be a good reason not to go with that firm.

Ask them some questions in their field to which you already know the answers. See if you are pleased with their response.

You should check on anybody who claims to have an answer to every question you have. Beware of someone who is a know-it-all. On the other hand, if you ask whether the advisor knows much about your business and the answer is "no," don't waste your time. Leave.

A red flag should pop up when an advisor tells you that your undertaking is "simple." One woman, interviewing a group of attorneys at one of the most prestigious firms in the industry, was alarmed when they cheerfully advised her that she had no problems with her proposed undertaking, despite the major obstacles that frequently loomed in her complicated business. "Your name and your reputation will pave the way for you," they assured her.

She immediately sought out another firm. The team she interviewed there told her, "It's expensive. It may fail. We may encounter litigation, which we love—but it may cost you $100,000 if the worst case happens. Are you sure you are willing to take that risk? It may take years instead of months. And after we've spent tons of your money, you may still fail. Go home and think about it and let us know."

She went home, buoyed by their candor in telling her all the potential problems—which she was already well aware of. She hired them and pursued the project.

One way to test the difference between two firms when you are uncertain which is better: Give them both the same project and evaluate the way they each handle it.

Check Them Out.

When you find advisors you think are smart, ask for the names of some of their clients with businesses similar to yours. Visit the other clients and see how well you think they are doing and how similar their circumstances are to yours. If everyone in your line of business is prospering mightily with the advice of the accountant or attorney you are considering, it is a very positive sign.

Which Is Better for You—an Individual or a Firm?

Generally a group of advisors, a firm, is more appealing than a solo operation. If you go to one person in practice, you are totally dependent on that attorney or that accountant, and you get only what they know. One person cannot know everything. And when your lone lawyer is not in the office, you are up the creek. There is no backup available for you.

A small firm is generally better for your business than a huge one. "Small" is one with 10 to 100 attorneys or accountants; they have experience that is available to you as you need it.

A large firm, one with more than 150 accountants or attorneys, may not be best for you. A huge firm may have many huge clients who overshadow you.

Margaret Booth, who heads a New York public relations company, first selected one of the giant accounting firms. "It was a mistake," she declares flatly. "We were nothing to them. We're now with a small firm where we are valued."

Having a senior partner do all your work can be unnecessarily costly. The more senior they are, the more they cost. In a medium-sized firm, having a junior partner assigned to you may mean a financial savings. If the junior partner is able easily and professionally to handle your work, you do not also need to involve the higher-priced senior partner. A good firm will assess your needs and determine which rank of seniority is adequate to assist you.

A firm may also have a team of specialists in other fields; thus, as your problems change, they can provide you with different experts without your having to change firms.

The Relationship is Not a Marriage.

While there is much to be said for having affiliations with your advisors that span the years, don't treat the relationship as a marriage. *You* pay the bills. You can leave any time you want to. If your company grows rapidly, you might find you have outgrown the attorneys and accountants who were adequate when you founded it. Perhaps while you were growing, they were standing still. Such breakups can be emotional, because advisors sometimes look upon their long-term clientele as captives. Don't be captive. Go for the advisors who can best service your company's growth and survival.

Your Advisors Should Be Compatible—But Not Pals.

Your advisors should respect each other and work together as needed. But more important, you do not want your accountant and attorney to be too chummy. You would do well to choose two advisors who have as little as possible in common to provide yourself with divergent sources of information. You should definitely avoid teams of accountants and attorneys who routinely work together.

Ideally, they will have gone to different colleges, be of different ages, and not belong to the same social organizations. The independence of each of them can be of great benefit to you when you encounter problems in your business. Between the two of them you should have access to broad experience and many perspectives.

If the two are friends who went to the same school and go to the same country club on Saturday night, they might be far more reluctant to disagree with each other. If they are friends, they could fall in the trap of saving face for each other—perhaps at your great loss. With advisors, you are always the one who pays the greatest price.

When Your Advisors Disagree.

When your tax attorney and accountant disagree, one of them is wrong. When you find out which, fire the culprit. Unfortunately, when you are given conflicting advice you yourself have to decide which you think is right—unless you decide to bring in a third expert.

"Don't Worry" Is the Worst Advice You Can Get.

Whenever someone tells you, "Don't worry," *it's precisely the time you ought to start worrying.*

Beware unrealistic claims such as, "None of my clients have ever been audited," "All of my clients get refunds," and, "I've yet to lose a case."

"It's important to understand that paid advisors are not necessarily right," says Kate McGrath of KM Media Productions. "There are good, bad, and mediocre people in every walk of life. You don't have to do what they say—your instincts count."

You should not necessarily believe in authorities. You must take the responsibility yourself for the decisions made about your business. The experts give you their advice. You should treat them merely as sources of information. *You* make the decisions.

Negotiate Fees.

Don't be shy. Ask about the fee. Don't hesitate to bargain it down to a lower price. Most advisors charge an hourly rate for the time they spend with you or working on your business, but many of them will negotiate their fees. "I end every conversation with my advisors with a discussion of their fees," notes designer/retailer Dianne Benson.

CHAPTER TWENTY-ONE

Your Credibility and Your Business Grow Hand in Hand

The most critical ingredient of success is that you must be excellent at what you do. The first step is to develop a product or service of which you are proud. Until you've got your ducks in a row you want to keep a very low profile.

When you have your act together you are ready to focus on building a fine reputation and a loyal clientele.

"In any business, a shoe factory or a law office, the problem is always how do you get business. You certainly don't get it by going in your bedroom, closing the door, and hiding under the covers," notes attorney Joan Ellenbogen. "You've got to go around, be seen, join things, present yourself. The men know how to do it. They know how to entertain customers. If two companies have two equal products and you invite the customer to a basketball game, the customer is going to go with the one who invites him. Women don't do that as much as men do."

You should target who your audience is for your goods and

services and build a strategy to reach them. Your market may influence many choices you make: how you dress, what charities and clubs you belong to, the leisure activities you undertake. To the extent that you are willing, you can integrate your life into your business. Or you can do it the other way. You can choose a business that permits you to live your life precisely as you like. The choices are yours to make.

But Excellence Is Foremost.

The most important ingredient of success in any undertaking is the excellence you bring to it. There is no substitute for attention to detail, attention to your customers, and reliability. Being superb is integral to any success in business. If you try to fake it, you probably will never have a business that will be successful.

But excellence in itself is not enough. If you are wonderful and sit in a closet and never let anyone know, you will probably fail despite your expertise. To be successful as an entrepreneur you have to make the right contacts.

Your Contacts Are Critical to Your Success.

The lifeblood of your business is in your contacts. This is true in any business. To build a network of contacts you must work constantly so that you interact with both your key suppliers and your key customers often enough that the definitions between "friends" and "business associates" blur. You may entertain for business reasons frequently and enjoy it thoroughly, since your associates often become your friends. There may be only a few people in your life who are not "contacts" for something.

You must always be on the alert to new business opportunities. You must carry your business cards with you. You must not let your customers take you for granted. You want them to rely on you year after year and recommend you heartily to their own business contacts.

Referrals Are Essential to Some Businesses.

In some professions, such as law and medicine and architecture, and in some businesses, such as consulting and retailing, word of mouth is an important part of building a successful business. The only way to get referrals is to have satisfied customers who tell all their friends and associates about you.

Respect from your peers is also important. Impressed by your consistently high performance, they recommend you to some of their customers. They know that because you are excellent, anyone they send to you will be impressed by their judgment.

If your business relies solely on referrals, it may be slow when you first begin, and you will need patience in the formative years.

Try to cultivate as diverse and wide a referral base as possible. The broader your base, the more secure your future.

How to Woo Your Customers.

Customer relations may be a crucial aspect of your success. The care and feeding of your customers is extremely important. If you do it well, the good will you establish may provide a cushion to persuade a customer to stay with you when things beyond your control have gone wrong.

Think of client relations as a long courtship. Treat your customers as you wish your favorite person would treat you.

Tips for Wonderful Client Relations.

In General

Offer your client a beverage when he/she visits your office/store. Remember (file) names of spouses and children. Ask about them.

Remember (file) birthdays and wedding anniversaries with flowers or note.

Include a thoughtful gift with the delivery of a large order.

Help your client in other ways. Have the "inside track" on restaurants and so forth. Keep your client "in the know."

Keep a file of past orders by client. Remember client preferences.

Add a special touch to everything you do, such as a ribbon on the portfolio, colored tissue paper on a package, a logo on your envelopes.

Make your client feel special.

Involve your family with the customer's family.

Only let your clients see you at your best.

Treat your clients as though you were wooing them for marriage.

In the Office

Hold the door for your client.

Hang up your client's coat.

Escort your client to the door. Special clients get escorted to the elevator or to their cars.

Stand whenever your client approaches you.

Seat your client before you seat yourself.

Give your client undivided attention. Let the client overhear when you arrange to "hold all calls."

Meet your client at the airport personally. Give him/her curb-to-curb service.

Entertaining

Take the client places where he/she will see people who are impressive.

Prearrange a good table.

Check out the restaurant before you take a client.

Take your client to an exclusive private club.

Drop your client off at the door before you park your car.

Let your client precede you behind the maître d' to your table.

Give your client the best seat.

Let your client be seated before you are.

Ask your client what he/she wants before you order. Order something similar to put your client at ease. If the client orders five courses, for example, you order five courses.

If service and/or the food are terrible, don't mention it. Perhaps the client won't notice.

Tip the coat check person for your client's coat.

Let your client wait inside while you get your car.

Having a High Profile Is Important.

In a business where you sell your own personality along with a product or service, you have to be available, conspicuous, and recognizable. You have to be highly visible.

A strong personal identity may be your most powerful selling point. It is hard to imagine Mary Kay Cosmetics having been so successful without the gregarious Mary Kay Ash at its helm. By the same token, it's hard to remember what the world was like before Diane von Furstenberg burst upon the scene, selling us everything from dresses to perfume.

But it isn't just the superstars who have to maintain a high profile to promote their products. It happens every day in every city in America. If you own a shop that bears your name, you usually show up almost every day, personally ministering to your customers. You cater to customers, attending to their needs and wishes. "The owner" is someone special to the customer. By the same token, you may own a restaurant and personally greet your diners every day. You may even do your own radio and television ads, personalizing your business as much as possible. Faith Stewart-Gordon, owner of the Russian Tea Room in New York City, personally writes and narrates delightful anecdotes which she uses as radio advertisements for her restaurant. Trained as an actress in previous years, she lends sparkle to the establishment's image.

You can create your own visibility. For instance, if you're a realtor, you can advertise in local newspapers, routinely including your picture in the ad. Potential clients will remember seeing your picture. You'll find it doesn't seem to matter that you paid for the publicity yourself.

The picture of Lillian Vernon Katz, of Lillian Vernon, appears routinely beside a brief letter from her included in the millions of mail-order catalogs her company sends out every year—a deliberate attempt to personalize her business. It works. Katz regularly gets bundles of letters from women she doesn't know. Sometimes they confide in her as though she were a personal friend. She answers each and every one, including the correspondence that arrives every month from a woman she has never met.

You can hire someone to be your image. If you want to open a dress shop without being a fashion plate yourself, name it something besides your name and hire a fashionable woman to operate it for you. Deborah Szekely, owner of the glamorous Golden Door spa, does not see herself as a glamorous person. She is short and has a hard time keeping extra pounds off, so she hired her image. She has blond, sleek, lean, tall management.

A high profile may be a burden. Once you've established yourself, it may be difficult for you to escape your creation. A woman who has created an image of beauty and glamour may be forced to be beautiful and glamorous all the time. One such woman on vacation, ill dressed and without makeup, darted out to the grocery store near her country home. Sure enough, the next day her picture appeared in a major fashion paper. Someone had snapped a photo of her as she got out of her car. "Sometimes this image business can get to you," she laments. "I envy women who don't always have to be perfect."

With visibility comes responsibilities, there is no doubt. If you own a restaurant, you may have to be on hand day after day being charming to people you don't care for. If you have a health or exercise spa, you may have to work out and watch your own weight religiously—your customers may taunt you if you don't.

How to Raise Your Profile.

Step back from your business and try to view it through the eyes of an outsider. Is there something about you or your company that might be interesting to other people? If you don't feel qualified to write an article yourself, hire a public relations expert or a ghostwriter to do it for you. That's what the heads of major corporations do.

Courting the trade press may be vital to business—particularly in cosmetics, fitness, antiques, design, and communications, to name a few. Free editorial coverage of your business, whether prompted by a public relations firm or not, can help you achieve a credibility that only intensive—and expensive—advertising might provide.

You may write articles and offer to be quoted in publications your customers and colleagues will likely read.

If you can't see what's interesting about your company, hire the most creative public relations firm in town to help you find some aspect of your business that can be turned into a newsworthy item for local and industry magazines and newspapers to broadcast for you.

Speak out on issues facing your industry. But speak only after carefully weighing the merits of your viewpoint. Try to be on the winning side. Mary Eileen O'Keefe, who heads up a coal consortium, testified before Congress on an issue. It was controversial, but O'Keefe spoke out on the side that was upheld and later made into law.

Local organizations provide an excellent opportunity for you to gain exposure throughout the community. If you want to raise your profile, join youth organizations—you'll meet parents. Don't hesitate to let the people at your church know what business you are in. Volunteer to help raise funds for the building committee—that would give you increased exposure to many of the larger businesses in town. The church benefits and you benefit, too.

You may join the board of an organization to keep up-to-date with current developments in your particular field. Bettye Martin, president of Gear Inc., notes that she is on the board of the Rhode Island School of Design and other professional organizations "because I want to keep up with what's going on in design and business."

Before you join an organization, consider precisely how useful the contacts you make in it will be to you. Don't limit yourself to women's groups, but don't exclude them, either. Don't limit yourself to industry associations: you need exposure to business people outside your area of enterprise. Exposure to a mainstream of the business community can be invaluable.

Whenever you volunteer to help an organization, be absolutely certain you have the time to see the project through. Just as you can make valuable alliances in organizations, you can, with ineptitude, lose important allies. Don't venture into uncharted territory.

Major Associations You Can Join to Raise Your Profile

1. National Restaurant Association, 311 First St. NW, Washington, DC 20001; (202) 638-6100.
2. International Franchise Association, 1025 Connecticut Ave. NW, Suite 707, Washington, DC 20036; (202) 659-0790.
3. Gift Association of America, 372 Park Ave. South, New York, NY 10011; (212) 696-9251.
4. American Hotel & Motel Association, 888 Seventh Ave., New York, NY 10019; (212) 265-4506.
5. Independent Insurance Agents of America, 100 Church St., 19th Floor, New York, NY 10007; (212) 285-4250.
6. National Association of Insurance Brokers, 311 First St. NW, Suite 700, Washington, DC 20001; (202) 753-8880.
7. National Association of Insurance Women, P.O. Box 4410, 1847 East 15th St., Tulsa, OK 74159; (918) 744-5195.
8. American Society of Interior Designers, 1480 Broadway, New York, NY, 10018; (212) 944-9220.
9. National Association of Manufacturers, 1776 F Street NW, Washington, DC, 20006; (202) 626-3700.

10. Direct Marketing Association, 6 East 43rd St., New York, NY 10017; (212) 689-4977.
11. National Association of Real Estate Brokers, 1101 14th St. NW, Suite 900, Washington, DC 20005; (202) 289-6655.
12. National Association of Realtors, 430 N. Michigan Ave., Chicago, IL 60611; (312) 329-8200.
13. Women's Council of Realtors, 430 N. Michigan Ave., Chicago, IL 60611; (312) 329-8483.
14. Association of Investment Brokers, 49 Chambers St., Suite 820, New York, NY 10017; (212) 269-6428.
15. American Society of Travel Agents, 4400 MacArthur Blvd. NW, Washington, DC 20007; (202) 965-7520.
16. American Accounting Association, 5717 Bessie Drive, Sarasota, FL 33581; (813) 921-7747.
17. American Association of Attorney-Certified Public Accountants, 24001 Alicia Parkway, Suite 101, Mission Viejo, CA 92691; (714) 768-0336.
18. American Society of Women Accountants, 35 E. Wacker Drive, Chicago, IL, 60601; (312) 726-8030.
19. American Women's Society of Certified Public Accountants, 500 N. Michigan Ave., Suite 1400, Chicago, IL 60611; (312) 661-1700.
20. Associated Antique Dealers of America (Cleo M. Forah, Pres.), P.O. Box 88454, Indianapolis, IN 46208.
21. National Association of Dealers in Antiques, RR6-5859 N. Main Road, Rockford, IL 61103; (815) 877-4282.
22. American Apparel Manufacturing Association, 1611 N. Kent St., Suite 800, Arlington, VA 22209; (703) 524-1864.
23. The Fashion Group (Apparel), 9 Rockefeller Plaza, New York, NY 10020; (212) 247-3940.
24. American Bakers Association, 1111 14th St. NW, Washington, DC 20005; (202) 296-5800.
25. Independent Bakers Association, P.O. Box 3731, Washington, DC 20007; (202) 223-2325.
26. Artist Blacksmith Association of North America, P.O. Box 1191, Gainesville, FL 32602; (904) 373-7811.

27. National Blacksmiths & Welders Association, c/o James Holman, P.O. Box 327, Arnold, NE 69120; (308) 848-2913.
28. American Business Women's Association, P.O. Box 8728, 9100 Ward Parkway, Kansas City MO 64114; (816) 361-6621.
29. American Entrepreneurs Association, 2311 Pontius Ave., Los Angeles, CA 90064; (213) 478-0437.
30. Center for Family Business, P.O. Box 24268, Cleveland, OH 44124; (216) 442-0800.
31. American Federation of Small Business, 407 S. Dearborn St., Chicago, IL, 60605; (312) 427-0207.
32. National Alliance of Homebased Business Women (Wendy Lazar, Pres.), P.O. Box 306, Midland Park, NJ 07432.
33. Associated General Contractors of America, 1957 E St. NW, Washington, DC, 20006; (202) 393-2040.
34. National Association of Women in Construction, 327 S. Adams St., Ft. Worth, TX 76104; (817) 877-5551.
35. Council on Employee Benefits, c/o Goodyear Relief Association, 1144 E. Market St., Akron, OH 44316; (216) 796-4008.
36. Florists' Transworld Delivery Association, 29200 Northwestern Highway, Southfield, MI 48037; (313) 355-9300.
37. National Caterers Association, P.O. Box 7643, 660 Underwood Ave., Akron, OH 44306; (800) 321-8626.

Look Like What You Do.

Both your manner and your appearance convey to your clients and bankers important information about you. You must analyze how they perceive you. You must develop an image that reinforces your professionalism.

The first and most fundamental way to elicit confidence is to look like you do what you do. If you are an attorney and you show up in blue jeans, your client's first reaction behind your back is going to be, "You wouldn't believe it if you met her, but everyone says she's a crackerjack attorney." That isn't exactly what you want to project, because your image has become the first hurdle you must transcend with a new client.

Attorney Marcia Goldstein concurs. "If you don't perceive yourself as a professional and act as a professional, you won't be perceived as one."

Looking professional may mean wearing a suit or jacket. Rena Tarbet, a star Mary Kay Cosmetics saleswoman, also avoids slacks. She dresses in suits or dresses, but she wears a blazer to all business meetings. "Jackets are powerful," states Tarbet. She also personifies glamour and success to the women she motivates to sell for her. She always wears an impressive amount of diamond jewelry.

The role of a big-city professional requires an image of elegantly tailored femininity. For instance, Margaret Booth, who heads up a public relations firm in New York, wears suits with silk shirts and often a pearl necklace. Everything she wears is top quality.

Your appearance can reassure your customers. Chomie Persson, who owns an equipment dealership, wears a wide variety of clothes, from pants to simply cut dresses. Whatever she wears, she is careful to convey a sense of neatness. Since an equipment shop is by definition full of clutter, Persson's fastidious personal style subtly reassures her customers.

An investment banker routinely wears very serious, very conservative suits and shoes with a severe hairdo. She looks as if she's come straight from central casting to play the part of an investment banker.

But under no circumstances, no matter how conservative your role, should you dress as though you were pressed out of a cookie cutter. *That's* one of the reasons you fled the corporate confines. "I can't stand the notion of wearing a uniform," notes Anita Miller, chairman of a new bank in New Jersey. "So while I am wearing a tan suit and a plain white blouse, notice the Navajo silver and turquoise ring. I asked myself this morning, 'Now what's going to be unique and individual about Anita Miller today?' "

Not only do you want to look like what you do, but you want to look prosperous. Sometimes it is advantageous to subtly convey your success, confides a broker. "I dress very professionally but very expensively. Everything about me is expensive. I wear an emerald ring, for instance, to a meeting. 'Oh, what beautiful jewelry!' the guy I'm meeting with says. I've already established myself as a very successful woman."

Even if you are not yet wildly successful, be sensitive to what your customers expect of you. If expensive-looking clothes would be a plus, dress as expensively as you can afford to. Invest in a few good pieces of jewelry. Wear only the real McCoy, even if it's real bone or real wood. Buy a good silk scarf. Carry an expensive briefcase. What does success look like? It looks expensive!

Your Image May Fluctuate.

You may have a different image from one day to the next. "I'm a business actress," admits a communications consultant. "I don't project a unilateral front. I give people what they expect."

How you dress may depend on whom you're meeting with that day. If you have a corporate meeting, you wear a conservative suit and blouse and dress so that a corporate executive will feel completely at ease with you as a peer. If you are spending the day working in your office, you dress more casually—but still in an unmistakably businesslike way. You don't want to be embarrassed if a client drops in on you.

You may be a chameleon, carefully assessing precisely what appearance will be most effective for you. The head of a public relations firm observes, "I'm much more conservatively dressed when I go to a client's office than I am when a client comes to mine. If in my own headquarters I'm a little offbeat from the corporate world, it's good. But I'm careful not to look out of place when I visit them in their offices."

"I think about who I'm scheduled to see that day and where, before I get dressed in the morning," says a venture capitalist. "If I'm meeting with bankers, I pull on something superconservative and rich-looking. If I'm meeting with a bunch of inventors, I dress more 'with it.' " When she sees disparate groups of people in the same day, she decides by a simple rule: "If people want something from me or provide me a serivce, they'll take me as I am. If I want something from someone, I dress to give them what they want." Thus, if she met with her banker and a group of inventors on the same day, she'd dress for the bankers: she wants money from the bankers; the inventors need money from her.

Your Image Includes Your Office.

The way your telephone is answered and the way your office functions is a *vitally important* part of your image. You want personnel who are businesslike, efficient, prompt, and friendly. Even if you have a large staff, you will be blamed for the poor manners of the receptionist. From the very bottom level of an organization to the top, you are judged by the performance of those you've hired to back you up.

Your office can be designed to help inspire confidence in your clients—although no matter how fancy the offices, if the staff does not act professionally, you are going to lose business. Generally, a fancy office is not as impressive to your clients as you might believe. It should be last on your list of priorities when you go into business. Your customers come to you because they have confidence in you and your people. Good professional performance can override the bad impression of a humble office.

It is important, however, that your office always look orderly and functional. Conference rooms and waiting rooms should be clean and well organized. Your staff should never display a sense of panic or harassment to your customers. Hysteria does not encourage confidence.

How to Elicit Confidence.

Your image does not stop with your dress and your trappings; it also lives in your gestures and mannerisms. Convey that you can deliver. There are many things you can do to make it easy for your customers to have confidence in you. Promptness, for instance, is important. Never be late. Try to be four minutes early. That connotes that you're organized and eager to do business.

Talk positively. Show enthusiasm. One consultant notes, "They've hired me because they think I know something they don't. I speak directly and state my ideas. I don't hesitate. I don't hedge. On the other hand, I don't want to be overbearing or pushy. I keep a pleasant, upbeat manner regardless. I never contradict a client in front of his peers. I'm being paid to make people look good, not cause them to lose face."

Being honest and fair from the very beginning also builds credibility. Doing your homework makes you look smart.

In many businesses clients are best reassured by constant contact with you and by being able to reach you. Often you may find that giving a customer your private telephone number may build confidence and security. If you do, be prepared to go the extra mile. Customers will sometimes call you in the middle of the night. "I keep my clients constantly informed, constantly hyped," says one businesswoman. "The sale does not end when they sign the contract. That's just the beginning."

How to Inspire Confidence

Act confident—regardless.

Dress "pulled together." Look like you've planned every detail. Wear the best.

Look tidy, clean, and well groomed. Wear bright lipstick.

Say, "It is . . ." not, "I think it is . . ." Be positive.

Look your clients in the eye.

Stand with authority. Speak clearly.

Thoroughly rehearse major presentations.

Have your facts at hand. Do your homework.

When you "don't know," admit it. Find out as soon as possible and tell your client.

Organize yourself in private before you meet with your client. Don't let him/her see you flustered or harried.

Whip out a good pen to take notes.

Carry a well-organized briefcase.

Charge what the market will bear.

Smile. Smile. Smile.

Shake hands with everyone: a firm, direct handshake.

Socialize with your clients.

Look like what you think the person you're with thinks you *should* look like.

Be four minutes early for all appointments.

Send related press clippings to the client to keep you in mind.

Talk directly about the business at hand.

Don't be shy about relating past or current awards and successes.

Always deliver more, better, and faster than you promise.

Telephone to assure customer satisfaction.

Drive a well-groomed car that projects your image.

Have a businesslike support system.

Work in an office that projects your image.

Be Sure Never To:

avoid looking your client in the eye

be late

fail to show up and not explain

leave your client waiting on a street corner

delay returning phone calls

procrastinate

let your bra straps show

let your slip show

wear run-down shoes

talk about how rotten your business is

chew gum

revise upward your initial cost estimate

totally lose your cool

show annoyance
fumble
shuffle
be hysterical
undercharge
wear dark glasses during the day
ignore your client
admit defeat
cry

You Can Be Your Own Woman.

One of the advantages of being in business for yourself, as opposed to working for a corporation, is that you are free to develop your own personal style. You can break all the rules and still succeed. No one tells you what to do. It's your decision.

Be your own woman. For instance, Georgette Klinger, the owner of skin care salons around the country, dares to be herself. "I refuse to be hemmed in. I'm very much an individual. I'm me," says Klinger, who isn't confined to people's expectations simply because she is in the beauty business.

You know your own circumstances, and it's up to you to define a unique personal style. Muriel Siebert, the remarkable woman who created a stir in 1967 by opening her own brokerage firm on Wall Street, takes delight in breaking the rules. She wears frilly clothes and bold prints—in a world where her peers dress with astonishing universal conservatism. Since Siebert, having ventured into what was previously an exclusively male territory, is indeed a maverick, the image suits her wonderfully. She plays it to the hilt. "It's an important part of my business. I play up to my image," she says. "I like bright clothes and purple dresses and suede pants suits. I like them and the press loves it. And it's me anyway."

Wendy Rue, founder of the National Association of Female Executives, Inc., is an energetic woman with short, pale blond hair and her own special style. "I don't conform," she declares. "I always wear white. I dress for attention. I don't want to be forgotten. I've always been that way. I didn't think I could measure up to the conventional look."

On the other hand, a woman who heads up a public relations firm only wears black. A designer never wears jewelry or scarves, maintaining, "The woman is the ornament." Another successful public relations chief dresses to look tall. "It's hard to be taken seriously when you're only five feet tall," laments the diminutive executive.

Having an image doesn't mean you're wedded to it. You can play with your image as you go along. A fashion designer is in the process of sophisticating hers. A communications consultant is buying a red Porsche to add some snap to her image. A high-energy management consultant is making hers more feminine and softer, slowly, in stages, so that she doesn't startle her clients.

One of the nice things about being in charge of your own destiny is that you can be yourself. There is only one absolute trait you have to embody to be successful: excellence. Everything else is negotiable.

Strategies for Moving Full Steam Ahead

Once you have a thriving company, a whole new world opens up for you. You can consider cloning your operation by franchising it. You can consider selling your shares and going public—essentially cashing in your chips. Once it is growing and profitable, your company becomes desirable to others. But it is impossible to be successful in business in today's competitive environment and not be exceedingly alert and in touch. Times change so fast that you, as a businesswoman, are forced to cope with change, constantly assessing the marketplace and your alternatives.

Plunging full steam ahead is the most exhilarating aspect of having your own company. But the plunge forward must be based on prudence, awareness, and due caution.

CHAPTER TWENTY-TWO

You Can Franchise or License Your Company

One of the alternatives available to help you expand your business is franchising. When you franchise you give someone permission to use the name of your business. You also train them and give them assistance in learning to run an extension of your concept in another location. In return they pay you a fee and some kind of ongoing royalty or percentage of their profits.

All this sounds easier than it is. Franchising requires a great deal of preliminary research and planning. You must first be certain your business is likely to be popular as a franchise and that you have the management resources to handle it.

When Are You Ready to Franchise Your Business?

If you want to franchise your own company, how do you know when the moment is right? There is really no hard and fast rule here. It's a matter of judgment on your part and on the part of the franchise experts you consult.

The most important factor in successfully franchising is not how long you've been in business but how prepared you are to proceed. Jack McBirney of the Franchise Consulting Group in Boston says of potential franchisors, "Ten years may be too soon and one year might not be soon enough. You have to have your management act together, retailing, marketing, your concept, and, of course, capital—everything in this world takes capital. We have to see an ability for you to grow. Loads of people can run one successful operation but don't have the ability to grow with it."

You need to learn to delegate and share responsibility. "You should not franchise if you can't delegate," says Carol Green, who owns Franchise Services of America, a company that helps other businesses franchise themselves. Green learned about franchising by running a highly successful franchise for Weight Watchers in the Rocky Mountain area.

What Kinds of Businesses Are Franchisable?

In order to have a cloneable company you've got to have a business that is marketable to potential franchisees. Says McBirney, "We look for concepts that are new or emerging, or an old concept with a new twist—mostly service or specialty retailing. Or we look for businesses that can be perceived to be fun versus a muffler shop or a hamburger stand. If a business has the aspect of fun, it has the potential to be hot usually, like Have A Heart in Boston. In five hundred square feet they sell everything with hearts on it. Also there's the Accelerated Learning Centers. They found a niche in special education for slow or disabled learners, now that school fundings have been cut back."

To be a viable franchisor candidate you need to have a unique-ness of concept, or of product, or of marketing and distribution. "The key is really the creation of an illusion. The carving out of a market is just *positioning* yourself. After all, how different really is

Wendy's from McDonald's from Burger King?" observes Carol Green. While one restaurant with a special cachet can spawn a successful franchise, another one, lacking that special something, might not.

Don't kid yourself. Not every business is suitable to be franchised. Some businesses simply don't lend themselves to it. Some areas, such as manufacturing, rarely have franchise candidates.

Whatever your business, you probably would not be able to market it until you've already proved it viable. If you want to franchise your coffee shop, you would do well to have at least one exemplary operation doing a thriving business before you begin to harbor hopes of franchising it.

There Can Be Advantages to Franchising.

Once you have a salable concept and a bustling prototype, franchising can help you expand your business in ways that might be impossible without it. For instance, if you own a business in Chicago, you can't adequately give personal service to customers at a New York branch office. "Franchising helps give you the ability to develop management-level people who have a vested interest in the outcome of the business," observes Carol Green. "It also gives the parent company an opportunity to develop auxiliary businesses. For instance, Weight Watchers developed a line of food because it had the capital to do it: it didn't have to shell out money in geographical diversification."

Indeed, well-managed franchising provides additional capital for you. You help your franchisees prosper, and fees and royalties are paid back to you.

How do you figure out what the value of a franchise of your business would be? There's no hard and fast rule. You first need do a lot of market research on what expenses you will incur traveling to visit potential sites, training the franchisees, and marketing. But you should not try to make a lot of money in the sale of the franchise. "Your goal should be to help make the franchise successful, because in the long run that's where the money is for you, too," observes Jack McBirney.

Would Franchising Work for You?

Franchising is not for everyone. Sometimes the magic is too personal to be cloned. Says Faith Stewart-Gordon of the Russian Tea Room, "This is a single enterprise. There are no franchises because this is such a personal business that I think it's impossible to be in two places at once."

Women in other businesses where a special atmosphere is critical to success agree. Says Deborah Szekely of the Golden Door spa in Escondido, California, "I turned down franchising even when I needed the money. You can't franchise the magic."

Sometimes franchising would undermine the atmosphere that makes your business so successful in the first place. Georgette Klinger opened skin care salons in several cities but still has no intention of franchising. The reason: She thinks the allure of pushing her skin products on her customers would be irresistible. As it stands, Klinger does not pay commissions to her employees for selling her products because she does not want them to be encouraged to sell customers unneeded products.

Moreover, franchising requires that you spend time and money outside of your basic business. You must evaluate whether the distraction is worth it to you. Dianne Benson, who has no intention of franchising her apparel shops, says, "I'm not interested in multiplying my store one hundred times in boutiques across the country. There would be too many people to deal with, too many details."

Licensing Can Expand Your Business.

Licensing is a very different process from franchising, but one you might consider if you are in the appliance, home furnishings, apparel, or home linens business—if and only if you have a name that would lend cachet to the products that use it.

To understand the typical arrangement licensing entails, consider one of the most successful licensing organizations in the country, John Weitz, Inc. Michael Wynn, president of John Weitz, Inc., is regarded as one of the savviest people in the licensing business. Wynn describes a John Weitz licensing arrangement using the Palm Beach Company as an example. "The Palm Beach Company, one of the largest manufacturers of men's tailored clothing, has been a Weitz licensee for seventeen years. They have the right to manufacture and market John Weitz blazers, suits, and sports coats. They have showrooms all over the United States, a huge sales force, and their own manufacturing facilities. Our input and contribution is the design and the right to use the John Weitz name on hang tags, labels, and in advertising—all subject to our approval. We receive a percentage of their net shipments of John Weitz merchandise."

The license period is usually from three to five years, with a renewal option. A percentage of the fees is paid upon execution of the agreement. The concept is very different from that of franchise fees. First, a payment schedule is agreed upon and partial payment is made. If there's any surplus over and above the minimum that is expected to be produced, it's paid at the end of the year, quarterly, or at the convenience of the people involved. Any other money due is paid later.

Licensing is very specific; for example, the Palm Beach Company is licensed to market and manufacture suits, blazers, and sports coats—but not separate trousers. It is also specific about territory. Licensed territory can be regional, national, or international, depending upon prior agreements with other licensees.

As a licensor you can exercise a right to check for quality control. But it is not a problem if you only deal with quality licensees— they also have their own reputations to uphold. Notes Wynn, "The Palm Beach Company has been in business for eighty years. It would be presumptuous of me to tell them how to make a suit. We have some thirty licensees. We can't know more about their specific category of business than they do." Before you grant a license, be certain that the company getting it is respected and experienced. You should deal only with the most reputable firms in your industry.

Licensing Is for After You Have Made It Big.

Licensing is not a business for Jeannies-come-lately. You need credibility on both sides. As a start-up you would be unlikely to have the name that any credible business would be interested in using. First you have to build your own reputation. For instance, if you are a young designer, you would have no possibility of being licensed until you first make a name for yourself. So you might initially apprentice to someone who is already successful, such as Diane von Furstenberg. During those few years you would work at building a name for yourself.

After you have proved yourself, the obstacles are less formidable. Comments Wynn, "The established design firms know that somewhere along the line young talent is going to leave anyway, so they say, 'Okay. We'll take a collection. You design it with your own name.'" After your name is established you are in a position to license yourself.

One of the reasons licensing is so attractive is that a carefully licensed name continues long after the individual has gone. The successful name becomes an institution of its own. The names of Anne Klein, Dior, and Chanel continue to provide vibrant showcases for generations of designers.

CHAPTER TWENTY-THREE

Everything You Need to Know About Going Public

After your business is established and operational, you may want to consider going public. That means you sell little pieces of your company, usually as common shares, to anyone who is willing to pay for them. Once you offer the shares in the marketplace, they are bought and sold by investors—usually strangers whose faces you will never see—at a price dictated by psychology of the stock market and the performance of your company.

Going public requires a determination on your part, because the road to the public auction place is arduous and likely to create more headaches for you than have yet been counted in the aspirin commercials you see on television.

Going Public Puts Money in the Till.

There can be spectacular results when you take a company public. You can really raise money—a lot of money. Andrew F. and Mary

M. Kay of Kaypro Corporation, based in Solana Beach, California, went public in August 1983 and raised a whopping $244.9 million. Monro and Henrietta Milstein, owners of the Burlington, New Jersey–based Burlington Coat Factory Warehouse, took their company public in June 1983 and raised $188.3 million. Lorraine Mecca's Micro D, a company she founded in Santa Ana, California, went public in July of 1983 and raised $32 million.

The money raised by Mecca for Micro D, a microcomputer hardware and software wholesaling company she founded in 1979, was an important cash transfusion, repaying debts and sustaining growth. Going public helped Mecca enter the ranks of big-time business. "I've never regretted going public," declares Mecca. "It's the smartest thing we ever did." Sales surged to $71 million in 1983, up from $3.5 million in 1980. Earnings leapt to almost $1.1 million from $415,000 during the same period.

Sandra Kurtzig went public with ASK Computer Systems, Inc., in 1981 and raised approximately $10 million. ASK, another California computer company, also took off. It is one of the fastest-growing publicly held software companies in the nation. Revenues for fiscal 1984 increased to over $65 million, 65 percent higher than the previous year.

There's no question that raising cash is a major reason to go public. If you want a fresh infusion of interest-free money in the corporate till, the public arena can be very appealing.

Going Public Impresses Your Bankers.

A major reason you might go public would be to raise an amount of money your banker would not loan you. After the public offering, your banker is likely to be far friendlier and view you with new respect.

Being public has a dramatic effect on how you are viewed. It eliminates the "Are you sure you are serious?" question that bankers often have when women approach them for loans. Being public is viewed as a testament to your commitment.

Once your company's shares are publicly traded, you have an objective reference point to use to value the worth of your company with your banker. If you can point to stock that is trading actively at $15, you can calculate your company's total worth in the marketplace. If the public believes your company is worth that much, chances are your banker will, too.

When your company is public it is forced by law to divulge its financial dealings. Such forthrightness gives you further credibility with your bankers, who seem to be more trusting if they know you have the Securities and Exchange Commission to face if you mislead them or the public.

Once you have a market for your shares, you and your employees are free to cash in your chips. You can more easily sell to the public than you might be able to otherwise. Moreover, selling off only a portion of your company is far more difficult privately than it is in the public marketplace.

Further, you may be able to sell a successful "hot" company for considerably more share by share to the public than you could get selling it all in one piece to a single purchaser.

Going Public Makes You a Star.

Going public can make you a star in financial circles. Often there are press lunches and meetings with bankers, money managers, and security analysts. You get to put your picture in your annual report and send it out all over the country—a nice ego boost if business is booming. If you are successful, going public means the business world can see precisely *how* good you are, since your financial successes are regularly revealed to the public.

Then, once a year you address your shareholders. You are in charge. You are on public view. If your business is successful, you get cheers and accolades after you deliver your speech.

In short, taking your company public lends glamour to your business presence. It focuses a spotlight on you as the woman behind the company. The mere thought of being able to take a company public elicits sighs of envious admiration from women whose privately held companies are off to a good beginning. "Wow. What a *coup* going public would be," says the owner of a small manufacturing company.

Going public automatically gives you national status. "It elevates the company dramatically. It takes you out of Mom and Pop status and puts you in the corporate league," says Dr. Diana Guetzkow, president and chief executive officer of Netword, Inc., a company located just outside of Washington, D.C., which Guetzkow took public in 1983.

Employees Can Benefit.

Going public not only earns points for you with your bankers, it may give you esteem and credibility in the eyes of your employees, too. Being publicly held may make your organization more attractive to top-flight talent as your company grows. Having a market value can engender a sense of pride and security among your employees.

Mary Wells Lawrence cited her employees as a major reason for going public with Wells, Rich, Greene, Inc., an advertising agency. She figured that stock participation would be an effective lure to attract some of the most talented minds in advertising.

It was a wise move. Lawrence had been a wunderkind in the advertising department of Macy's at twenty-three and had gone on to shine brightly in the advertising community, founding her own firm at the age of thirty-eight. When she took the company public two years later in 1968, it was already approaching billings of $100 million. The agency was riding high, and Lawrence was the talk of the advertising world. The popularity of the firm and the glamorous image that Lawrence, who sometimes weekended in Paris, brought to the company made the initial public offering a great success.

Going Public Means You Live in a Glass House.

Many of the gains you make from going public can also turn out to have downsides. Great visibility may reveal so much about your company that it becomes vulnerable. Notes John Westergaard, who heads a Wall Street–oriented research firm, Equity Research Associates, "You may not want your competitors to know *too* much about your business." If you are public, you may be forced to reveal information that will allow your competitors to read between the lines to steal your innovations and concepts and snatch your market share away from you.

You also become subject to intense scrutiny. You become fair game for financial writers and securities analysts. Once you take your company public you become part of the public domain. They have every right to dog your corporate footsteps and criticize your every move. The raves you get when business is booming become howls of outrage overnight if you make a false move. Further, shareholders have the right to question your every decision and demand an explanation for what you spend for X and Y. If you want to move to another location or a new facility, you have to expect several inquiries questioning your judgment.

You have to learn to watch what you say. You must carefully announce to the entire public any development in the company that will alter its prospects and affect the price of its stock. Anything you tell one analyst or writer that you have not told the world can get you into trouble. Since fortunes can be made and lost in the movement of your stock price, you have to learn how to deal with the press and the industry without revealing anything you should not. This can be exceedingly constraining.

Should you issue a projection of profits only to encounter misfortune that causes a reversal, be prepared to be tarred and feathered by those who have believed you. The more the press elevates you, the farther you have to fall, should your business turn sour. When you are private, you can bite the bullet, endure losses for a period of time because of long-term benefits you see for your business; but when you are public this is more difficult. The stock market likes profits. Investors usually think in terms of the short run.

Regardless of what happens, you can expect to be persistently questioned and second-guessed by outsiders. Lorraine Mecca, head of Micro D, recalls the early days of being public. "I got calls from what seemed like every analyst, every investor, and all the institutions. They kept asking me why the price of our stock was so low; and I just didn't know. I knew we were making a profit, but we hadn't announced earnings yet so they couldn't see it. When the quarter's earnings were finally released to the public and we were profitable, then all the phone calls stopped. Now it's down to a few calls a week. But you see, no matter what happens we get calls. Even if the price goes up, they call and demand to know why. And sometimes I just don't know."

You Are Required to Tell All.

Telling the whole truth and reporting it to the Securities and Exchange Commission on a continuous basis is an onerous task. Notes Dr. Diana Guetzkow of Netword, "You have a great deal more accountability." That accountability means you have to pay teams of accountants and attorneys to gather and process complicated financial and legal reports.

You have to furnish quarterly reports to each and every one of your shareholders. You are required to hold an annual meeting at which your public can tell you how intelligent they think you are— or aren't. You have to mail out expensively assembled annual reports and file a complex document every year with the SEC, outlining the progress of your business in a form the SEC requires. Further, you have to distribute proxy statements that report the salaries of you and your key employees. If you pay yourself too much money, you can receive flak from your shareholders and the general public. If you scrimp on your key people, it could encourage your competition to dangle fat compensation packages before your employees and entice them away. Moreover, adding up your salary, stock ownership, and bonuses, the public can estimate your net worth. If you are wealthy, charities will camp out on your doorstep.

The effort to compile all the required information a public company must file can be enormous. As your shareholder base expands, even the postage to mail all these separate notices can become an expensive item.

The costs of complying with the requirements of both Uncle Sam and the SEC must be taken into account before you decide to go public. You must pay attorneys and accountants hefty fees to keep you up-to-date with all the laws. You must hire writers to compose your copy, photographers to take pictures of you and your products, designers to lay out the reports to make them readable, printers to produce them, and suppliers for the paper itself. And don't overlook the expense of the time you and your key employees take to address analysts, give interviews, and worry about compliance.

The Price of Your Stock Can Plummet—and Stay Down for Years.

Once you are public you really have no control over the price of your stock. It not only has to do with how your company performs, but it has to do with how sexy your industry is. Wall Street watchers are notoriously fickle about the objects of their affection in the marketplace. It is possible that you can do everything right and your stock still may trade at rock-bottom levels.

Of course, the fickleness of Wall Street adds more stress to your life. The entire valuation of your company is based on how your shares do on Wall Street. It is a great frustration if you do everything right, the company shows a profit, and still your stock stays glued to the bottom. There's nothing you can do except try to persuade analysts that their trading departments should pay attention to you.

To enhance the value of your company you have to court the securities analysts who are experts in your industry. If this courtship is successful, it can add value to your company, as the analysts recommend your stock to institutions and stockbrokers, who then buy your shares. The burden of selling to Wall Street falls on you. There is nothing magic about being public that will automatically make top Wall Street talent love your business. You will have to seek out influential people and convince them of your company's worth.

If the price of your stock nose-dives, your key employees—whom you hoped to entice—may lose confidence in you and leave you, disillusioned by your failure to make their dreams come true.

Moreover, if your company is underpriced in the market, you are a natural takeover target, particularly if more than 50 percent of your shares are publicly held. Your shares are a bargain, so another company snaps you up. Then you will no longer be the boss: somebody else owns you—which may be precisely what you have always wanted to avoid.

If you make a mistake and investors get burned, it can be a long time before you can regain their initial confidence. After all, your problems cost them money. In addition, if the price of your stock is low, many investors tend to believe there must be a reason and that they just don't know it; and the lower your stock gets, the more apprehensive people will be about buying it. The frustrations of the marketplace can give you ulcers, even when you have everything else in your business in hand, because the stock market is something you can never control.

Who Should Not Go Public.

If your company is very small, it may not be worthwhile to go public. Below a certain point the legal accounting and marketing expenses can be so great as to make it futile. How small is too small? Generally if your company generates revenues of less than $5 million, you would have to be very unusual to make going public viable. If you're smaller, it may be almost impossible to get first-rate institutions even to talk to you.

John Jensen, Jr., vice-president and manager of the Institutional Syndicate for Merrill Lynch Capital Markets, says, "Merrill Lynch wouldn't take someone public for a deal of less than $15 million, but there are firms that would do a $500,000 deal."

"We prefer to do deals of at least $10 million," says Andy Blum, head of syndication at L. F. Rothschild, Unterberg and Towbin. "But of course there are exceptions, subject to who brought it in, the quality of the company, how interesting it is in our perception to the investment community, and if there are other corporate clients interested."

Where You Begin.

You start with a good accountant and attorney. "Good" means experienced in dealing with the SEC. "You need good counsel," says Cathy McCoy, associate director, legal, of the Division of Corporation Finance at the Securities and Exchange Commission in Washington, D.C. "Those who have never prepared registration statements before make mistakes—perfectly innocent ones, but they are time-consuming." You need good advisors not only to prepare your initial registration statement, but to respond to the SEC when it makes comments asking for additional information. Sometimes getting that information is "like pulling teeth," says McCoy. "The better the advice, the smoother it will go and the less costly it will be. Those with experience will charge more on an hourly basis, but their meter won't be running that long."

Under no circumstances permit your standard day-to-day accountants or attorneys to talk you into letting them take you public. Let them get their experience at somebody else's expense. If you are not willing to search for and find seasoned specialists to assist you, chances are you'll never make it over the SEC hurdles.

"The SEC has a good record of being aware that we pose or are perceived to pose hurdles," admits Cathy McCoy. "We don't want to prevent people from raising money, but we want to protect investors to make sure they have information to make their investment decisions."

It's up to you to provide that information. It's a formidable task. You are first required to file a registration statement with the SEC before any stock can be offered for sale. The registration statement must be deemed "effective" by the powers at the SEC before you can go public.

The registration form is in two parts. Part I is the legal offering or "selling" document, called the prospectus, which must be furnished to all purchasers of the securities. This document must be made available to everyone who offers to buy your stocks. Part II is a supplement you file with the SEC. You do not have to provide it for your investors. It is available to them if they want to go to the SEC to read it.

The entire basic registration form is called the S-1. Here are some of the items the SEC requires:

A description of your company's business
A description of the company's properties
Material transactions between the company and its officers and
 directors
Competition
Identification of officers and directors and their remuneration
Certain pending legal proceedings
The plan for distributing the securities
Your intended use of the proceeds
Detailed requirements concerning financial statements which must
 be audited by an independent CPA

In addition, you are obligated by the SEC to provide any other information necessary to complete the S-1.

Factors that make you a risk, such as the lack of a track record, adverse economic conditions in your industry, a lack of market for securities you want to sell, or a dependence on key personnel must be featured prominently in your report. These items are usually listed near the beginning of your write-up. Its function is to insure that investors in your company have enough information to get an honest break. "The prospectus says, 'You guys could really lose your shirts,' " says Dr. Diana Guetzkow.

Part I, your prospectus, is more difficult to compile than the supplement because it is not a fill-in form, but is written in a narrative style. You and your advisors must succinctly and accurately—and with no holds barred—describe your company. It can be a low-cost effort, or you can print it up on glossy paper and include pictures.

How Long Does It Take?

Generally you can expect it to take three to six months from the time you begin to fill out the forms to the time your offering is cleared by the SEC.

It takes from one to three months to fill out the forms—after you decide on your accountants and attorneys. You can be stymied if you pick weak advisors. Notes Elizabeth Brandon-Brown, president of Quest publications, who became disenchanted with her accountant during the form-filing process, "Midstream we had to switch accountants. If there's any advice I have to offer, it is to ask around to other companies that have gone public for recommendations for accountants and attorneys."

After you've got the right advisors and give the S-1 to the SEC, it can be weeks or months before you win their approval and can get clearance to sell stock.

Choose Your Underwriter Carefully.

While you are searching for the right advisors you also need to shop for an underwriter to take you public. Your underwriter is a brokerage firm who agrees to represent you in the stock market. It buys some of your stock for resale to its clients and arranges a large network of other brokerage firms to buy other chunks of stock until all the shares you are selling are accounted for. (Your underwriter may also be referred to as your "investment banker.")

Going public has its own vocabulary. The network is a "syndicate," and lining up the network is called "syndicating." Your broker is the "syndicator." The commitments made by other brokers to buy and sell your stock are called "subscriptions." When all of your stock is pledged for, you are "fully subscribed."

Underwriters evaluate your company in terms of its size, its maturity, its potential growth rate, and whether it is regional, national, or international. They also want an offering with enough money involved to attract major institutions like banks and pension funds, who have billions to invest. If you can demonstrate excellent quality and substantial size, blue chip underwriters such as Shearson/American Express, Merrill Lynch, and E. F. Hutton may pay attention to you.

If your company is already well established and profitable, your chances of securing a first-rate underwriter are excellent. If you are still a start-up operation, you should look for venture capital to sustain you until you can attract a solid, reputable underwriter. Otherwise you may be forced to deal with small-time hustlers who may make more out of the deal than you do.

"Unless you've got one of the top blue chip underwriting companies, they're just criminal," declares a woman who went public with second-rate underwriters.

When you're shopping for an underwriter, you should talk to several before you decide on one—or two—to handle your move. "Look at the deals an investment banker has done before," advises John Jensen, Jr., of Merrill Lynch. "Look at how actively the stock of a company they handled has traded, how much it's gone up in the period right after it was offered, how actively the firm has made a market, whether it's been able to make secondary offerings, and the research coverage with the firm. When you look at the ownership of that company, it should be pretty widely spread out. Optimally there should be institutional holdings."

"One of the things to look for is an underwriter who has done a number of underwritings," advises William D. Witter, who heads up a New York investment management firm bearing his own name. "You can find that out in the SIA (Securities Industry Association) handbook. It tells who the underwriters are, how many salesmen they have, how much capital they have, and how many deals they've done. I think you need to be sure of getting your money. So you need an underwriter with a lot of salesmen, because in a good market these issues are not hard to sell, but in a down market or on a down day, you need to have salesmen who can really put it out—otherwise you run a serious risk of not getting your money." (The SIA is located at 120 Broadway, New York, NY 10271.)

Your underwriter should be familiar with your industry. When you interview them they should ask the right questions about your company. *If they don't understand your business, they can't sell it*. You should sell yourself along with your business—when they are backing your company they are really backing you as well.

Do as Elizabeth Brandon-Brown of Quest Publications did: "We called the comptroller of companies our potential underwriters had taken public before. We asked about how they handled it, if they were fair, what kind of commission rates they were charged, and what kinds of problems they had with their underwriter."

The smaller and less established you are, the harder it is to get underwriters even to talk to you. "I easily talked to one hundred securities firms, and they all told me to mail them something and then they never read it. Of the one hundred you'll get meetings with ten percent, and out of those only one will be interested. And if they're interested, they'll string you along with ten other deals," relates Dr. Diana Guetzkow, who took a fledgling company public.

Is One Underwriter Enough?

Should you use one underwriter, or should you use two or even three? You would be wise to choose more than one, because each of them will have different strengths. Moreover, if you start out with two, you have one as an insurance policy in case you and the other one disagree and part company.

Naturally, any investment banker will urge you to let it be the sole underwriter. "Frankly, I think you should never use more than one. It creates a lot less confusion, and they can really focus on you without competing with the other guy," says John Jensen, Jr., of Merrill Lynch. "We're obviously not averse to having co-managers, but we prefer to do it by ourselves."

Having only one underwriter might be the preference of someone in the underwriting business, but someone who is not disagrees. William D. Witter, whose firm does research and investments but does not do underwriting, observes, "Investment bankers are like merchants. They want to sell all of it, not just part. Their preference is to do the whole deal and a big deal. So they will lead you away from using co-underwriters if they can, and they'll lead you into a bigger deal if they can—the bigger the deal, the more money they make."

Alternatives If Your Company Is Small.

If your company is still small, there is an alternative to the complex S-1 registration. You can file the S-18. This is a simplified form available to your company if you want to raise less than $5 million from the sale of your company's securities. The S-18 requires less complex reporting. It also requires less time and money to receive permission from the SEC to sell stock in your company.

How the S-18 differs from the S-1:

Where the S-1 requires three years of audited financial statements, the S-18 requires only two.
The narrative description of your company is shorter and less detailed.
You can deal with your regional office. Says the SEC, "The primary advantage of a regional filing is that regional office personnel may be more familiar with local economic conditions, the busi-

ness community, the financial environment, and in some cases the background and history of the company."

Cathy McCoy of the SEC says, "Now you don't have to fly across country or run up your phone bill."

Regulations A and D are also aimed at helping small businesses sell shares to raise money. Regulation A is a "conditional exemption registration form for certain public offerings, not exceeding $1.5 million in any twelve-month period." You file an offering statement with your regional office. The offering statement, after it has been approved, must be given to everyone who buys a share. The main residual advantage of Regulation A is that no periodic financial reporting is required by the SEC if your company has assets of under $3 million and fewer than five hundred people have bought your shares.

Regulation D offers the applicant three different ways to go public, depending on how much money is involved. None of the securities sold under this regulation can be resold by shareholders within two years of purchase.

Rule 504 permits sale of up to $500,000 of stock in a given twelve-month period; if you qualify, you receive an exemption from the expensive reporting otherwise required.

Rule 505 permits you to raise up to $5 million. You can sell shares to thirty-five "nonaccredited" people and as many "accredited" ones as you like. "Accredited" means either a very wealthy individual or a bank or institution that has enough sophistication to understand the risks involved in investing in your company.

Rule 506 is for even larger offerings. But even your "nonaccredited" investors have to receive an SEC-approved prospectus on your company.

Regulation D is large and complex, but well worth the time it takes for you to investigate it to see if you qualify. It could provide you with interim financing until you have grown enough to make a splash when you plunge into the larger public marketplace.

Regional Offices of the Securities and Exchange Commission

NEW YORK (Region 1)
New York Regional Office
26 Federal Plaza
New York, NY 10278
(212) 264-1636

BOSTON (Region 2)
Boston Regional Office
150 Causeway St.
Boston, MA 02114
(617) 223-2721

ATLANTA (Region 3)
Atlanta Regional Office
1375 Peachtree St., NE
Suite 788
Atlanta, GA 30367
(404) 881-2524

CHICAGO (Region 4)
Chicago Regional Office
Everett McKinley Dirksen Bldg.
219 S. Dearborn St.
Room 1204
Chicago, IL 60604
(312) 353-7390

FORT WORTH (Region 5)
Fort Worth Regional Office
411 West Seventh St.
Fort Worth, TX 76102
(817) 334-3821

DENVER (Region 6)
Denver Regional Office
410 17th St.
Suite 700
Denver, CO 80202
(303) 837-2071

LOS ANGELES (Region 7)
Los Angeles Regional Office
5757 Wilshire Blvd.
Suite 500 East
Los Angles, CA 90036-3648
(213) 473-4511

SEATTLE (Region 8)
Seattle Regional Office
3040 Federal Building
915 Second Avenue
Seattle, WA 98174
(206) 442-7990

WASHINGTON (Region 9)
Washington Regional Office
Ballston Center Tower 3
4015 Wilson Blvd.
Arlington, VA 22203
(703) 235-3701

The Vocabulary of Going Public

Public Offering—	Selling shares of your company to the general public.
Equity—	Stocks, interest in a company that is offered for sale to the public. There is an element of risk attached.
Securities—	The same as equity.
Institutions—	Banks and pension funds. Any money that is managed for a group of people. The opposite of institutional is individual.
Private Investors—	Investors in your company who are solicited individually, not publicly. Usually they agree not to sell the equity in your company to anyone else.
Window for Going Public—	This is the auspicious moment picked by your underwriter to open your stock for trading in the public arena. There is no magic formula to predetermine this day. The right window is largely a guess and a hunch.
Capital Formation—	Raising cash.
Registration Statement—	The complex document required by the SEC before you can receive permission to go public.
S-1—	The number of the registration form often used to refer to it. S-1 is the section of the Securities Act—the Bible of the SEC.
SEC—	The Securities and Exchange Commission, the watchdog of the public marketplace. It is usually referred to by its initials. Occasionally it is called "the Commission."
Retailers—	The brokerage firms that distribute and sometimes tout and sell stock

	in your company to individual investors.
Subscribed—	An agreement of a network of retailers, corralled by your underwriter, to commit themselves to buy chunks of the stock you are offering, which they in turn sell to their customers. Your stock is "oversubscribed" when a demand for it exceeds supply. This is a happy circumstance: when the market in your stock opens, its price usually responds to the demand and goes up immediately.
Underwriter—	A brokerage firm that agrees to help you take your company public. You may have more than one. Your underwriter helps you generate interest in your company and sell your stock to the marketplace. A classy underwriter can be of great assistance in making your public offering a success.
Investment Banker—	In this context, another way to refer to your underwriters.
Syndication—	Your underwriter is the syndicator. It is responsible for forming the network of other firms around the country to buy your stock and sell it to both retail and institutional clients.

The more entities that own your stock, the "wider its distribution."

Strategies for Completing the Business Cycle

After you have led your company through the full cycle of business activity, growing systematically, there are still some final decisions to be made. For instance, you might decide to sell. But selling out is not as easy as it sounds. If the deal is not put together right, you may find your buyer is having difficulty paying back the full amount promised. So you buy back your company to build it up again.

Then again, you can't run your company forever; at some point you must face the decision to retire. This issue is one that should be dealt with long before you are actually ready to retire, because many of the decisions made years earlier will affect the ultimate outcome of your ownership.

Finally, if you have taken your company public, because of changing stock market conditions you may make the decision to go private again. It's difficult, but it can be done.

CHAPTER TWENTY-FOUR

Retirement

Think about Retiring.

Even if you are young and own a little business that is doing well, someday that company may be substantially larger and you may be thinking about retirement. You should keep your future in mind now while you are building the company. Will you sell it? Will your children take it over? Should you bring in a younger person and train him or her over the years to run it for you when you retire?

Much of the success of your future lies in your taking a long-term view. Even though the day-to-day operations may be hectic, don't let them distract you from planning your future. The ground-work should be laid well in advance of the day you retire.

Just as your business has succeeded because of your careful and continued planning over the years, you must also plan for the ultimate transition: leaving the business. This could be disruptive and destructive unless you lay your plans carefully in advance.

You do not want to carelessly undo the results of years of work.

If you intend to retire and let your business continue to operate, supporting you and your family, you want to be sure it will continue to prosper. If you intend for it to continue even after your death, supporting your heirs, you must plan for this well in advance. If you desire to sell your business, you want to be certain it will not fall apart as soon as you are gone, because successfully consummated sales are often contingent on continued postsale performance.

In any of these instances lack of forethought about what will happen to your company when you leave it can give rise to enormous difficulties.

First, Incorporate.

If you incorporate, your company has a life of its own separate from you. Should you sell out, retire, or die, the company is intact, continuing on without you. It has the same corporate seal and identity number, the same banking relationships. If you have not incorporated, passing on your company can be more complicated.

Plan for the Succession.

Long before you retire or approach old age, you should recruit managers who will be capable of running the business in your absence. You should groom them carefully over a period of years, gradually increasing the breadth and depth of their responsibilities. You should instruct them in your philosophy of business until you feel assured these managers share your goals and objectives. You do not have to be secretive about your formula for success; since you control the stock of the company, you need never worry about being usurped.

Once you have planned for succession, and your designated

successor has proven his or her capabilities, let your choice be known both to your employees, your clients, and your suppliers. If you have groomed your successor carefully enough, no one will be surprised or dismayed.

Also announce your plans for future company ownership and control to everyone involved with your company. You should personally deal with the uncertainties and insecurities of your employees and clients long before you hand over the reins. People tend to fear the new and the unknown. You are best qualified to reassure them. Many of your final arrangements for your succession will entail hand-holding and reassuring various key individuals.

What to Do If Your Family Will Continue to Be Involved in the Business.

If family members have proved themselves to be interested in your business and capable of running it, you may decide to turn it over to your heirs to run.

Once again, be up front from the beginning. If there are several members involved, let them know first of all that only one can be president. Try to build a team, stressing the unique skills of each member. To avoid political infighting, be candid about the apparent prospects of each one from the beginning. As soon as a front-runner emerges, his or her presidential capabilities should be clearly apparent to the others. Give your candidate opportunities to demonstrate a knack for running your business.

As soon as you feel certain which heir should run your business, announce that decision. If you want to solidify the front-runner's position, you can write your will to back up your decision. Since it is your company, you can allocate its stock after your death in a way that will reinforce your choice. You can also announce the terms of your will to erase any doubts there might be as to the finality of your decision.

Under most circumstances, you would not actually turn over stock in your company to your heirs before your death. As long as you live, you would do well to hold all the stock yourself—or at least a majority position.

How to Settle Your Estate When Your Family Is Not Interested in Your Business.

You could hire a management team to run the company and leave the stock to your heirs. But often the first thing that happens after the death of a company founder is that the family puts the company on the market for sale to the highest bidder. Usually the price they fetch is less than what you could garner while you are in charge.

The best time to sell a company is while it is profitable and active and you are still its life force. If your family has no aptitude or interest in your business, sell it off yourself and will them the money instead of the business.

If the company is such an important part of your life that you do not want to relinquish it until you are absolutely unable physically to continue, negotiate a sale that permits you to continue on as CEO for as long as you desire.

Whether you sell for stock, cash, or deferred payments to your estate is entirely dependent on your individual circumstances. You and your expert accountants should plan intensively before any sale is consummated.

Do Not Act in Haste.

Planning the ultimate outcome should not be a sudden or rushed process. Soon after you establish your business you should begin to consider the possibilities of what it can mean to your life and possibly to that of your children. Decisions made many years before you contemplate leaving can influence your conclusions about its final outcome—whether to bring your family into the company, for instance, or the extent to which you delegate its management.

In arriving at the most judicious disposition of your company, you may need to bring to bear all the expertise that made your company a success in the first place. You, an entrepreneur, will no doubt approach the termination of your role in the same straight-forward way you approach most business decisions. Let's face it, if you balked at making decisions, you wouldn't have become an entrepreneur in the first place.

CHAPTER TWENTY-FIVE

Selling Out

After you have built your business, nurtured it carefully through growth and diversification, and devoted years of your life to it, the day may come when you want to sell it. There are a variety of reasons why you might decide to divest. One might simply be that you are tired of the company's problems, even if it is profitable. "Some days I think I'd *give* the business to someone," quips a successful realtor.

Selling your business may be a stepping-stone for you. Most sellers go on to start another venture, frequently using the expertise acquired in building one company to be even more successful in another.

Why Would You Sell?

One reason you may sell is to cash in your chips. If you balk at the nuisance of going public, selling is your only alternative to get the full amount of money your company is worth.

As an entrepreneur you always thrive on challenges. Once you have established your company, you may find the challenges are diminished and the thrill is gone. Perhaps you get bored coping time and again with the same problems you have encountered from day one. "When I am very cranky and suffering from jet lag, I think about selling," notes the head of a company that has annual revenues of over $100 million. Boredom is the most common reason business owners decide to sell out.

You may sell to get out of a mistake. If a company is not doing well, it can be tempting to get whatever money you can and let someone else invest his or her ideas, capital, and energy.

Sometimes the very success of your company can be the thing that prompts you to sell. When your company grows larger than you ever dreamed, you may discover that much of the fun has disappeared. The bigger the company, the more you are relegated to managing personnel and mountains of paperwork—but as an entrepreneur you may detest the administrative side of business. On the other hand, you may be frightened at handling a large company all by yourself. If you sell it, you can start off small again and put money in the bank. Incidentally, bankers are much more generous to a second venture once your track record demonstrates that a previous one succeeded.

Quite often a company is sold because none of its founders' children have an interest in running it. And there are other reasons to sell, less happy ones. Occasionally businesses are sold to liquidate assets so they can be divided to settle a divorce agreement.

The best time to sell is when your business is going very well, of course. A flourishing company can command a far greater price than one that is troubled.

Should You Have a Broker?

Business brokering is a fast-growing industry.

As a seller you have different considerations than the buyers in chapter 11 when it comes to deciding whether or not you want a broker. The bottom line is that, just as you give up a percentage of the sale of your house to your realtor, you also pay a percentage of the transaction to a broker who sells your company for you. The fees vary depending on the size and desirability of your business. Remember that these fees can be negotiated, too. Unless your circumstances are unusual (for instance, a key employee who knows the business inside out wants to buy you out), a professional broker may be a good solution for you. With a good broker orchestrating a deal for you, it is less likely to come unraveled.

Edith Hamilton, who has started, bought, and sold several beauty salons in Indiana since 1938, recalls that when she sold her first shop in the 1940s, it was "simpler then." Says Hamilton, "Even so, I didn't get a good deal on it. I didn't get the money I should have. Now it's even more complicated and I used a business broker the last time."

The best way to find a broker is to employ a strategy similar to the one described in chapter 20 for choosing an accountant and attorney. Ask for references from previous owners of businesses that have been successfully sold. Interview brokers to find one you are comfortable dealing with.

How Can You Tell If a Broker Is Any Good?

There are not many good business brokers around who will handle a business of $5 million or under. You may have to make many phone calls and conduct a number of interviews before you find a professional, experienced, qualified business broker who can be of significant benefit. There are several red flags to warn you the broker does not have the breadth of experience you need:

1. Beware of realty brokers moonlighting as business brokers. Selling houses is *not* the same thing as selling businesses. A realty broker may not know as much about assessing the difficulties of a business as you, the person who built up a viable enterprise and sold it in the first place.

There is no law against realty brokers selling businesses and even advertising business opportunities, thus the burden is on you to eliminate the ones who can tell you nothing of any real value.

2. If a broker has a standard one-page contract—usually a modified real estate contract—take heed. Businesses are complex. A sales transaction for a business is too complicated to be detailed on one page. For instance, David Goldfarb, head of Corporate Investment Business Brokers, Inc., says his firm's sales contracts routinely range in size from fifteen to fifty pages.

3. Don't trust a broker who says it is not necessary to consult an attorney. Although you don't want attorneys to call the shots in your business deal, you still need their legal input. The sale of a business is, after all, a legal transaction.

What If You Can't Find a Good Broker?

Since there are not many qualified business brokers interested in handling small businesses, you may not be able to locate one if your company is small. If you can't find a professional broker who has substantive information to give you and skills to contribute, you're just as well off proceeding alone. Simply consult an excellent attorney and carefully feel your way through the problems of your former business yourself. But don't *lean* on your attorney—*you* are the business person, not your lawyer—arm yourself with good advice before you act.

Your Business Should Have a Desirable Appearance.

Once you have decided to sell, you must keep in mind that your business is going to be surveyed by people unfamiliar with your undertaking. You want to show it in the best possible light.

The most important thing you can do is to continue business as usual.

Once you've made the decision to sell, you might lose some of your motivation and be tempted to be lax about pursuing your business. This can be dangerous. "I've seen deals fall apart after preliminary agreements have been reached because the shelves become bare or the hours the business was open decreased. Sellers should spruce up their business so it looks good," observes Massachusetts-based broker Tom West.

While you are putting your business in order it is not necessary to take care of every loose end. There's no reason to solve all your business problems before you sell your company, because anyone who buys it probably has different ideas about how to improve it. Says West, "They're not satisfied if the business has no flaws. It's just human nature to want to improve on it, to say, 'Gee, if I fix this up, add this line or this service and extend the hours, I can increase the business. . . .' "

Still, appearances do have an important psychological effect on potential buyers. If your business is located on the wrong side of the tracks and looks run-down, you may have difficulty selling it even if it's doing very well. On the other hand, a company located on the right side of town with an attractive façade is likely to be sold with ease—even if its business is not going well at all.

You May Need to Revise Your Financial Sheets.

Your company's balance sheet may be the most powerful vehicle for communicating its desirability to a buyer. But you may have to rethink your entire financial record-keeping system. If the only financial records you have are aimed at appeasing Uncle Sam, they can be misleading to prospective buyers. The business may not appear as profitable as it should. You want to present your financial operations in a way that makes it easy for prospective buyers to see what the true worth is.

You may have used depreciated values and taken deductions

because the tax laws permit it, but such figures may not represent the true worth of the business. "Reconstruct the profit and loss statement," advises Tom West. "Pull out the items that don't belong there. For instance, you didn't really have to go to Italy to check the price of salami if you own a pizza joint." You should organize the revised business analysis of your company so that prospective buyers can understand what the actual profits are.

The most important aspect of presenting your company favorably may be showing the difference in the amount of compensation (direct and indirect benefits) a professional manager would be paid versus the amount that you as a successful business owner have been drawing from the business. Once the company limousine, the company plane, the expenses for you and your spouse attending ten conferences a year—three of them overseas—the first-class plane tickets, and your generous expense account have been removed, hundreds of thousands of dollars would automatically drop to the bottom line.

Being Clandestine Can Be Counterproductive.

After you have several prospective buyers lined up, you should not be secretive about your intentions to sell. They are likely to sniff around and "spill the beans" anyway. You want to reassure key employees that the transition will be orderly. You may even opt to protect them by giving them employment contracts that continue after you have sold the business. Finally, your buyers may want your employees to guarantee the operation will continue to run smoothly after your departure.

You should discuss your imminent sale with your landlord. You want to know what kind of lease the buyers will be able to secure.

You should also discuss your intentions to sell with your key customers, assuring them of continued quality and service. "If 75 percent of your business comes from Sears, you want to make sure Sears will stay with the buyer," advises broker Tom West. "The thing is, you want to eliminate all the surprises. You don't want things coming out later that will blow the deal."

Finally, you should be straightforward about why you are selling your company. If you tell your buyers you're selling because a divorce made it necessary and the buyer finds out you are not married, the deal will fall through. Be honest about your reasons for selling.

If you are sick of the business, be candid about it. If you have problems you are tired of grappling with, admit it. If business is rotten and you don't have the energy to rectify the situation, be absolutely up front with the buyers. Or if business is excellent, but you've ultimately become bored with the sameness of the daily dramas, be frank about that, too.

How to Set a Price for Your Company.

There is a general rule of thumb in setting the price of a business: After you have reconstructed your profit and loss statement and eliminated all the items that wouldn't be there if the company was run by professional management, you will have a better feeling for what the actual profits are. The sale price will generally be about three times the annual profit your company makes.

Moreover, the value and attractiveness of your business is in the eye of the beholder. Your company may be viewed by prospective owners as a vehicle for mushrooming sales. In that case the company may be far more valuable to them than it is to you. Price it according to the perceived value and not to what it is worth to you, its jaded owner.

The worth of your company varies from industry to industry. "Talk to people in your industry," advises New York investment banker Patricia Cloherty. Your business can command a far higher multiple of its earnings when the industry you are in is "hot." Right now service businesses are selling well.

However, when all is said and done, businesses are as individual as houses. The prices they garner alter with timing and the psychology of the people you sell to.

How Much Cash Can You Expect?

Under nearly every circumstance, the sale of your company is unlikely to provide you with instant cash, as you might expect.

You may harbor dreams of having a lovely windfall when you sell your company. Don't get carried away. Typically, you will receive only about one-third of its total worth up front. "Two-thirds is too much. Ideally we like to see 35 percent," says broker David Goldfarb. (Don't forget you have to pay taxes on that down payment, which reduces your profit even more.) The balance of the payment for the company is usually remitted in the form of a promissory note, normally due within two to ten years.

Incidentally, the average sale price for businesses in the United States is roughly $90,000, according to one organization that tallies business sales. That means the average down payment is $20,000 to $30,000—a nice bundle, but not enough to make you rich.

You Can Help Someone Buy You Out.

If you very much want to sell your business and you have found a buyer who seems the right person to continue it, you can arrange seller financing—you finance the person yourself. Approximately 90 percent of all privately held businesses are sold this way. If you find the ideal owners and they don't have enough money to buy your company, you could let them pay you off over a period of time, assuming you think the company is going to continue in operation and the buyers can make it work. Don't be greedy; make the terms reasonable. Arrange the terms of the payout so that the cash flow of the business can absorb it.

The interest rate you should charge your buyers doesn't relate to the rate the banks charge, because if you finance the sale, the bank never gets involved. Through all the years when interest rates soared, seller financers still stuck to the range of 10 to 13 percent interest for buyers of their firms. Otherwise the deals likely could not have survived.

Frequently, to sweeten a deal, one side may throw in a house, car, or boat in lieu of cash. If you report it, it is perfectly legal. Says broker David Goldfarb, "In many cases it's not such a bad idea. When there's an exchange there can be tax advantages to both parties. If people trade two things of equal value, there's no tax consideration."

Remember, however, that no matter how experienced an entrepreneur you think you may be, when you decide to sell you may be up against one of the most challenging undertakings of your career. You need good advisors. The acumen you have garnered over the years will be an important asset in negotiating the buyout of your company. *Be cagey and be tough.*

You Might Have to Buy Your Company Back After You Have Sold It.

Suppose you sell your company, thinking you are finished with it. You pursue another business or sit back and wait for the installment payments to be made by the purchaser. Then you have a rude awakening—the person you sold the business to cannot handle it, and the business is faring badly. Most likely you sold the company expecting to be paid over a couple of years, but if the purchaser cannot generate adequate profits, he or she will be unable to repay you. You and your company's buyer become disenchanted with each other, and the buyer might want out.

In order to be able to obtain the sale price your company was originally worth, you may be forced to step back in to take charge of the remains of your once thriving business. You buy back what is left and then set about rebuilding it.

Why Might the Sale of Your Business Collapse?

The reason the sale of the business you used to own might fall through varies depending on the size of your company. If its value was under $5 million, the single most likely factor is that the deal was badly structured. As the owner of a company with relatively small sale value, you probably had a hard time attracting first-rate advice. It is extremely likely that the exact nature of your business was not effectively communicated to the person who bought it. Thus, the sale failed.

If your company's value was over $10 million, its sale may have collapsed for exactly the opposite reason: the transaction may have been doomed by an overdose of advice. The large profits involved in the sale of a big business prompt attorneys to descend like locusts upon buyer and seller alike. Unfortunately, most attorneys are students of law instead of business, and they may have little insight into exactly what makes a business run. Thus, they may advise things that are not practical for the company. They may also impose so many restrictions on the sale that the buyer is hampered in the day-to-day workings of the business.

Should You Use a Business Broker When You Rebuy?

It may seem to you that since you built the business you know it, and that it cannot have changed significantly in the few months or years since you sold it. Wrong. Think again.

Under the management of buyers who did not understand the business or could not cope with its demands, everything in your former company may have changed. The company's customers may be gone, their suppliers may be cynical. The inventory may be bad or depleted. Where once there was good will you carefully nurtured, there may now only be bad. There may be problems so large even you cannot comprehend them.

Moreover, your perception of the business may be distorted because of your previous involvement. You need an objective opinion.

Don't try to be a know-it-all. This is one time you definitely need a professional business broker—a good one.

CHAPTER TWENTY-SIX

Going Private After You've Been Public

Going public does not have to be forever. Under certain circumstances it is possible for you to buy back your shares and become a private company again. Sometimes going private after you've gone public is the most intelligent thing to do.

Wall Street Sets the Stage for You.

The circumstances that allow you to go private again are usually miserable. Generally, your company's stock has fallen totally out of favor on Wall Street and the price plummets, despite the company's excellent performance. Your shares are a terrific bargain. Unfortunately, being such a bargain, your company becomes a sitting duck for someone else to make a bid for your shares and take control. Instead of waiting for that to happen, you take the initiative and buy the shares back yourself.

Such was the case with Mary Wells Lawrence after she had taken Wells, Rich, Greene public for all the right reasons (see chapter 23). She experienced the fickleness of Wall Street firsthand. Initially her company was a darling of the marketplace, the toast of the town, trading up to $26 a share. Then, in 1973, the entire advertising industry fell out of favor with Wall Street. It was an unsettled period economically, (the OPEC embargo had rocked the foundations of monetary structures, and Wall Street did not trust anything without quantifiable hard assets). Since an ad agency's assets leave its offices every night in the elevator—smart people are an agency's chief asset—Wall Street shunned them.

Wells, Rich, Greene, a hot issue only a couple of years before, traded at a mere $5.50 per share in 1974. Lawrence, chairman of the company, opted to go private—again, for all the right reasons. She made an offer to buy up to 1.4 million shares for $3 in cash and $8 in principal subordinated debentures, a total value of roughly $7.75 per share.

Just as you might encounter under similar circumstances, Lawrence met resistance. Some shareholders had no doubt purchased her stock at over $20 and were unhappy to take such extreme losses. As frequently happens on bids to go private, complications arose. Shareholders balked at the price Lawrence offered and filed a shareholder suit against the company. It took three years—after the company agreed to pay some shareholders $22 for their outstanding shares—to complete the metamorphosis from public to private.

You Can Benefit Greatly from the Transaction.

Although some of your shareholders can get stung when you decide to take your undervalued company private, you yourself do not necessarily suffer. With the case of Lawrence, the net result of her taking the company both public and private was that in six years she doubled her percentage of ownership of the company—even though she had previously sold off large chunks of stock that earned her millions of dollars. And as chairman of a private company, she was free of fears of a hostile takeover.

Going Private Requires Expert Planning.

Should you find yourself in the position of going private, just as when you go public, you must surround yourself with top-notch attorneys who are experienced in managing these transactions. The moment of making the offer can be intense. Your boardroom will resemble a war room for weeks before and after you make the bid.

One of the major dangers of making a public offer to buy back your shares is that you are announcing to the world that you believe your company's stock is a bargain. Experienced company snatchers may jump into the fray and counterbid, offering a higher price. You and your bankers must be prepared to outbid them if necessary. You and your attorneys must be prepared to outmaneuver any predators. The battle can be intense and bloody. Going private takes canniness and determination, but it can be done: successful entrepreneurs have plenty of both.

Conclusion

The fact that the possibility of going public and then private again interests you is an indication of how far women have come. Twenty years ago these possibilities seemed inconceivable for us. But America is changing at a rapid pace and more and more of us are running larger and more successful companies. Lured by the freedom of being completely in charge as well as the prospect of financial success, the self-employed woman is indeed the wave of the future.

After all, we've now come a long way. We've coped with the possibility that corporate life, regardless of the security blankets it provides, may not provide us with the range of freedom or opportunity to accommodate us as women.

We've learned not to rush headlong out into our own undertakings but to plan ahead and then move in carefully planned steps to minimize the risks we take and our vulnerability to failure. How to start small and grow. How to attract the kind of personnel who can provide the best support system for our venture and how best to form alliances with partners and colleagues. How best to structure the business to enjoy the maximum rewards from our labors.

Of course, it has been necessary to do a great deal of homework, learning the buzzwords to comfort our bankers and forearming ourselves with enough financial and accounting knowhow to be able to avoid the obvious pitfalls. It is also wise to consider a full range of options, whether to start from scratch, to buy a franchise and use the experience of the franchisor's team to maximize your potential, or to buy an independent business outright.

Assuming excellence and prudence, and armed with smart advisors, you will find that you can do it—eureka, your company really works! You discover that you are in fact very good at what you do. That you can earn substantial respect in the business community. That your perseverence and canniness in the marketplace ultimately win you a significant credibility. Eventually you will discover how soul satisfying it is to have accomplished even more than you set out to do.

But as your venture grows and develops it is important that you expand your business only to a size as large as suits your own temperament and needs. If you want a giant company, go for it. On the other hand, if you are happy with a tiny boutique, don't let anyone bully you into expansion. Furthermore, if you want to sell out and retire or start over, you can. The choices are all yours.

After all, the whole point of being entrepreneurial is to expand your options. With the extraordinary control you exercise over your life when you are your own boss, you are finally truly free to be your own woman.

Appendix

What to Include in a Business Proposal for Your Bank

Description of business—Do not expect that your banker already understands your business. Describe it succinctly. Explain what it is, how it is viable and where its profitability lies. Explain what makes the business attractive. Cite examples of similar successful businesses and pinpoint the reasons for their success.

Financial prospects—Develop estimates of how much revenues and profits you expect the business to generate each quarter for the first two years. Give these on a quarterly and yearly basis. Don't tie yourself into excessive expectations. Project conservatively and leave yourself some leeway. Remember that if you outperform your original estimates you gain credibility with your banker.

Long-term expectations—Estimate on an annual basis what you can expect in three, four, and five years.

Cash-flow projections—Outline how you plan to sustain your venture on a month-to-month basis. Itemize safeguards you have to assure that you collect your receivables. Break down your expected profit margins.

Start-up costs—Document your estimates with examples of similar businesses in the area. Do your research before you talk to your banker. Estimate how long you expect it will take you to recoup your investment.

Market survey—Specify who your competition is and who your customers are. Define exactly how your operation fits into the marketplace. Your confidence and knowledgeability can be an important factor in persuading your banker to back you.

Marketing plans—Define exactly how you are going to attract your clientele. Include any advertising plans. Use examples of how similar marketing strategies have worked in the recent past in similar circumstances.

Uniqueness of your product—Describe what you can provide that sets you apart from your competition. Demonstrate how your product has been well received in the past or in another area.

Cost competitiveness—Compare your product to that of the competition. Cite examples of how similar products have been well received.

Your capability to run the company—Describe very positively your past successes in related areas and any experience and qualifications that demonstrate your ability to make the business a success.

Determining the Cash Flow of a Business

Be Realistic About Your Start-up Costs. Don't Underestimate Them.

Be sure to include:
>   special fees and licenses
>   insurance costs
>   equipment outlays
>   deposits and prepayment on leases
>   inventory costs
>   start-up legal and accounting fees

+ _____

> total the above
> (Add 20% to cover miscalculations)

Figure the Costs of Running the Business on a Monthly Basis	Money Scheduled to Come In Each Month
rent utilities secretarial and stationery car maintenance and gas salary inventory—nail down whether you must prepay or can pay later	*Receivables*—never assume money will come in simply because it is owed you

+ _____   + _____

> total the above   total the above
> (add 20% to allow for the
> unforseen and unexpected.)

IF

This Total . . . . Is Higher Than . . . . This Total
Money Has to Be Siphoned into the Business
or
You Have a Cash Flow Crisis.

Tips to Help You Meet Your Projected Monthly Cash Income Projections

Give incentives for prepayment—e.g., a discount for prepaying a year's membership in a health club.

Give your customers incentives to pay promptly for services already rendered—e.g., a discount if paid within 15 days.

Give incentives for cash payment.

All big projects should be paid for by the customer in installments—including an up-front payment.

Don't rely on a single customer for your livelihood. Expand your client base. That way you are not in dire straits if one stiffs you.

Get credit references on your customers—*before* they owe you.

Be cautious about opening charge accounts or accepting checks for products.

Contract with a credit card company and let them be responsible for collecting.

Never assume fancy people and big corporations pay their bills promptly.

Sample of Profit and Loss Statement
For a Shop Owner or Manufacturer
Statement of Operations
For the Period from January 1, 1986, to May 31, 1986

Gross sales		$102,500
Less: Sales discounts, allowances or markdowns		2,500
Net sales		100,000
Cost of goods sold:		
Inventory—beginning	$ 4,000	
Purchases	30,000	
Direct labor	20,000	
Payroll taxes and fringe benefits	2,500	
Rent	3,000	
Other direct product costs	2,000	
Depreciation	2,000	
	63,500	
Less: Inventory—end	4,500	
Net cost of goods sold		59,000
Gross profit		41,000

Operating expenses
  Selling:
    Commissions $ 8,000
    Advertising   5,000
    Entertainment and other selling costs   6,000   19,000

General and administrative:
    Office expenses   5,500
    Telephone   3,000
    Accounting   1,500
    Insurance   1,000

Total operating expenses   11,000   30,000

Net income before owner's salary and taxes $ 11,000

Courtesy of: Siegel, Mendlowitz & Rich, P.C., Accounting Firm

Sample Profit and Loss Statement
For a Service Business
Statement of Operations
For the Period from January 1, 1986 to May 31, 1986

Gross fees $100,000

Direct costs:
  Salaries $ 50,000
  Payroll taxes and fringe
    benefits   8,000   58,000
Gross profit   42,000

Operating expenses
  Selling:
    Commissions $ 8,000
    Advertising   5,000
    Entertainment and other
      selling costs   6,000
                                                         19,000

  General and administrative:
    Office expenses   5,500
    Telephone   3,000
    Accounting   1,500
    Insurance   1,000
                                                         11,000

Total operating expenses   30,000

Net income before owner's salary and taxes $ 12,000

Courtesy of: Siegel, Mendlowitz & Rich, P.C., Accounting Firm

Index

Canary Cafe, 124
Capital, 60, 63
    inadequate, 167–68
    initial requirements, 61, 63
Capital-intensive, 61, 63
Carr, Claudia, 39
Carswell, Dot, 186
Cash, amount that can be expected in
    selling out, 271
Cash cow, 60, 63
Cash flow, 60, 63, 281–82
    in avoiding bankruptcy, 167–68
Cash management, and financing, 80–
    81
CCI Communications, 191
Century 21, 37, 130, 132–33, 186
Children, hiring as employees, 184–85
Cibelli, Jessie, 38
Clark, Ann, 40, 201
Clark, Merry, 27
Client relations, 215–17
Cloherty, Patricia, 106, 270
Clothes, for meeting with banker, 66
Collateral, 71–72, 75
Collections, prompt, in avoiding
    bankruptcy, 169–70
Commission, broker's, 125
Communication with employees, 180–
    181
Compatibility with advisers, 210–11
Compensation, deferred, 179
Competition with previous employer,
    158–59
Computers
    and growth, 202
    instead of employees, 102–3
Confidence, eliciting, 222–24, 226–
    228
Contacts, and growth, 214–15
Contract
    franchise, 139–40
    with partner, 109–10
    for working in tandem, 114–15
Control over job, lacking in business,
    30–32
Cooperative, quasi, 115–16
Corporate Investment Business Bro-
    ker, 267

Corporation
    being smarter than boss in, 34–35
    criticism and stress in, 32
    defeminizing life in, 28–29
    discrimination against women in,
        26–28
    dreariness of salaried jobs, 29–30
    energy waste in, 32–33
    job vs. family responsibilities, 33–
        34
    lack of control over work in, 30–31
    subchapter S, 193–94
    See also Business
Cost
    of benefits for employees, 175–79
    of buying business, 126–27
    fixed, 59, 62
    franchise, 138–39, 143–45
    hidden, 56
    one-time, 62, 63
    overhead, 59
    start-up, estimating, 53–55
    variable, 59, 62
Creative Environs, 52, 191, 194, 198–
    199
Credit
    revolving, 72, 75
    terms, 72–73, 75
Credit cards
    for employees, 175
    financing with, 79
Criticism, and stress, 32
Customers, wooing, 215

Debt service, 72, 75
Deferred compensation, 179
Delegating to employees, 182–83
Delphi Stained Glass Centers, start-up
    costs, 143
Design Interiors, 86
Devanna, Mary Anne, 27
Dick, T. W., 124, 199
Disagreement among advisers, 211–12
Discounts for employees, 174
Distress signals, stress, 150–51
Diversification, growth through, 201–2

Image
in eliciting confidence, 222–24
fluctuating, 224–25
and office, 225
Income, meeting monthly projections,
281–82
Income statement, 74, 75
Incompetent employees, firing, 181–
182
Incorporating, 188–91, 192–93
before retirement, 260
Individual Retirement Account (IRA),
177
Insurance
for business, 194–95
health, for employees, 176
life, 74, 75
Inter-America Foundation, 203
International Franchise Association,
133
Interview with advisers, 208–9
Inventory turnover, 60, 62
IRA, 177
Isolation, combating, 91–92

Jackson, Kate, 185
Jacobson, Anita, 198
Jensen, John, Jr., 247, 250, 252
Job
keeping while going to school, 163
as training ground for own busi-
ness, 158, 160–62
Jones, Judith, 174

Katz, Lillian Vernon, 69–70, 175, 185,
218
Kay, Andrew F., and Mary M., 239–40
Kaypro Corp., 240
Kennedy, Jeanne, 131, 184
Kirby, 164
Kitchen skills, as basis for business,
38
Klinger, Georgette, 24, 34, 185, 228,
236
Klinger, Kathryn, 185
KM Media Productions, 102, 212

Knowledge of advisers, 206–7
Ku, Adora, 106
Kurtzig, Sandra, 240

LaBonne Cuisine, 40, 201
Labor-intensive, 61
Language. *See* Vocabulary
Lasky, Ella, 150, 153
Lawrence, Mary Wells, 242, 275–76
Levenson, Rustin, 115
Levine, Honey, 37, 132–33
Lewis, Bev, 164–65
Lewis, Harriet Gerber, 185–86
Licensing, and growth, 236–38
Life insurance, 74, 75
for employees, 176
Lillian Vernon, 218
Liquid Paper, 200
Lison, Kathleen, 131
Lists, 153–54
Loan
amount needed, 64–65
persistence in seeking, 69–70
and size of bank, 68–69
Lynn Wilson Associates, 191

McBirney, Jack, 135, 140, 234, 235
McCoy, Cathy, 247, 253
McDonald's Corporation, start-up
costs, 144
McGrath, Kate, 102, 212
McLain, Patti, 37
Malcom, Laurie, 26
Margin, profit, 59, 62
Market, targeted, 74, 75
Marketing, 61–62, 63
Market research, 198
Martin, Bettye, 78, 105, 201, 219–20
Mary Kay Cosmetics, 27, 155, 158,
165, 197, 217, 223
Mason, Jean, 39–40
Mason, John, 40
Mattis, Flora, 163
Mecca, Lorraine, 240, 244